Jefferson's G[...]
by Timberlake Werten[...]

CW00457631

First performed at Watford Palace [...]

Cast (in alphabetical order)

Christian	David Burnett
James	Burt Caesar
Daniel/ Mason/ Perrault	Gregory Gudgeon
Jefferson/ Carl Christian	William Hope
Susannah	Mimi Ndiweni
Sally/ Betty	Carlyss Peer
Harry/ Madison	Joseph Prowen
Martha/ Nelly Rose	Julia St John
Louisa/ Imogen/ Patrick Henry	Anna Tierney
Chorus	Full Company

Creative Team

Director	Brigid Larmour
Designer	James Button
Lighting Designer	Prema Mehta
Movement Director	Shona Morris
Musical Director	Catherine Jayes
Dialect Coach	Helen Ashton
Casting Consultant	Scott Le Crass
Deputy Stage Manager	Rachel Williams
Assistant Stage Manager	Emma Ryan

With thanks to:

The John Simon Guggenheim Memorial Foundation,
University of Virginia Library, Georgetown University,
Elizabeth Wertenbaker Mackenzie, Margaretta Wertenbaker
Roe, Jeanie O'Hare, Maria Aberg, Karl Sydow and Adrian Noble.

Cast Biographies
(in alphabetical order)

David Burnett Christian

Theatre credits include: Best Years of Your Life (Nabokov, Watford Palace Theatre); West Side Story (Warwick Arts Centre); Pioneer (curious directive, Norwich Playhouse) and Gate 32 (Gate Theatre).

In training: All My Sons; Three Sisters; The White Guard and Julius Caesar.

Burt Caesar James

Burt's work in theatre includes: Lopakhin in The Cherry Orchard and Noises Off (Birmingham Rep); Romeo and Juliet (Lyric Hammersmith); Crusade (Theatre Royal Stratford East); My Children My Africa (Watermill, Newberry); Macbeth (New York); Fanny Kemble (Nuffield, Southampton); Blood Knot (Latchmere); Eden (Riverside Studios); (Royal Lyceum, Edinburgh); Meridian in Blues for Mister Charlie and In Self Defiance (Sheffield Crucible); Serious Money (Royal Court, West End and New York); Brutus in Julius Caesar (English Shakespeare Company); Black Ey'd Susan (Croydon Warehouse); Judith (Glasgow Citizens'); The Merchant of Venice (Chichester); The Tempest and Strange Fruit (Liverpool Everyman and Playhouse); The Miser (Cambridge Theatre Company) and Moon on a Rainbow Shawl (National Theatre).

Work as a director in theatre includes: former Associate Director (Royal Court); Sidepockets (Theatre Royal Stratford East); Cloud Nine (Contact Manchester); Back Street Mammy and All God's Chillun Got Wings (West Yorkshire Playhouse); My Goat (Soho) and The Brothers Size and Yerma (RADA).

He has directed on film Remembrance by Derek Walcott and Welcome Home Jacko by Mustapha Matura for the National Theatre Archive.

Gregory Gudgeon Daniel/ Mason/ Perrault

Theatre includes: Wendy and Peter Pan (Royal Shakespeare Company); Travels With My Aunt (Menier Chocolate Factory); Equally Divided, and Time of My Life (Watford Palace); Blue Remembered Hills (Chichester); Sleeping Beauty (Birmingham Rep); As You Like It, Merry Wives of Windsor and A New World (Shakespeare's Globe); Cyrano de Bergerac (Manchester Royal Exchange); The Firework Maker's Daughter (Told By An Idiot); The Lion King (Lyceum Theatre); The Street Of Crocodiles (Complicite, tour); Le Morte D'Arthur (Lyric Hammersmith); Metamorphosis (Contact, Manchester) and Too Clever By Half (The Old Vic).

Television: Midsomer Murders, The Bill and Bergerac.

Film: Finding Rin Tin Tin (NU Image). Esther Kahn (Magic Lantern), A Pin For The Butterfly (Channel 4 Films).

Writing: Translation of Hisashi Inoue's Greaspaint (Lyric Hammersmith & Chijinkai, Tokyo); Amerikafka (Prague Shakespeare Co.).

William Hope Jefferson/ Carl Christian

Theatre includes: This May Hurt A Bit (Out of Joint); 7 Year Itch (Queens Theatre); Doctor of Honour (Cheek by Jowl); Twelfth Night (Sheffield Crucible); Swim Visit (Donmar); Miss Julie (Phoenix Theatre); The Cherry Orchard (Manchester Royal Exchange);The Normal Heart (Royal Court/Albery); The False Servant (Gate Theatre).

Film Includes: The Whistleblower; Walking With The Enemy; Sherlock Holmes; The Lady; Captain America – First Avenger; The Walker and Aliens.

TV includes: The Syndicate; Spooks; Episodes; Burton and Taylor; Upstairs Downstairs; Holby; Lewis; Midsomer Murders and Marple.

Mimi Ndiweni Susannah

Theatre credits include: This Is Not An Exit
(RSC); The Taming Of The Shrew (RSC); Hamlet
(Richard Burton Company); Sky Hawk (Clwyd
Theatre) and for the Midsummer Mischief
Festival: I Can hear You, Revolt She Said, Revolt
Again and Ant and Cicade (Royal Shakespeare
Company).

Film credits include: Jack Ryan: Shadow Recruit
(Paramount Pictures); Tarzan (Warner Brothers) and Cinderella
(Warner Brothers).

Carlyss Peer Sally/ Betty

Carlyss trained at RADA.

Theatre credits include: Hamlet (Shakespeare's
Globe Theatre UK and USA Tour); A Midsummer
Night's Dream (Shakespeare's Globe Theatre),
But I Made You a Mixed Tape (Etcetera Theatre);
The Rivals (UK Tour and Theatre Royal
Haymarket) and Les Liaisons Dangereuses
(Salisbury Playhouse).

TV credits include: Holby City (BBC); Eternal Law (ITV); Silent
Witness (BBC); Doctors (BBC) and Missing (BBC).

Joseph Prowen Harry/ Madison

Joseph trained at LAMDA. Theatre credits
include: An Ideal Husband (Chichester Festival
Theatre); Love and a Bottle (LAMDA/Out of
Joint); Sweeney Todd, The School of Night, A
Midsummer Night's Dream, A Few Good Men
(LAMDA); Mojo and Dinner (Acorn Productions)
and The History Boys (Oxford Triptych Theatre).

Television includes: Casualty (BBC).

Films include: The Ivory Year (short).

Joseph won the Highly Commended Award at the Spotlight Prize
2014.

Julia St John Martha/ Nelly Rose

Julia trained at LAMDA.

Theatre includes: The History Boys (Crucible Theatre, Sheffield); The Seagull (Southwark Playhouse); Our Father (Watford Palace Theatre); The Archbishop's Ceiling (Southwark Playhouse); The Madness of George III (West Yorkshire Playhouse and Birmingham Rep); The Three Sisters (Chichester Festival Theatre); A Tale of Two Cities (Cambridge Theatre Company); Nana for Shared Experience (Almeida Theatre); Larkrise (Almeida Theatre) and seasons with New Victoria Theatre, Newcastle Under Lyme.

TV includes: The Brittas Empire; GBH; A Question of Attribution; The Grand; The Victoria Wood Show; Gone to the Dogs; The Glass; Harry Enfield and Chums; The Blackheath Poisonings; Poirot; The Line of Beauty; Julian Fellowes Most Mysterious Murders; A Place of Execution; A Touch of Frost; Lewis and Casualty.

Film includes: The Young Victoria and Jab Tak Hai Jaan.

Anna Tierney Louisa/ Imogen/ Patrick Henry

Anna trained at Drama Centre London.

Theatre includes: Our Country's Good (Out of Joint); Follow: A Confusion About Her Solidity (Lux Associate Artists); Kolbe's Gift (Leicester Square Theatre); As Is (Finborough Theatre); After The Rainfall (curious directive, Norwich Playhouse, West Yorkshire Playhouse and Plymouth TR2); Tull (Bolton Octagon); Without External Ignition (Flipping the Bird/ Theatre 503); Brightest and Best (Pilot Light); A Cure For a Cuckold (The Sam Wanamaker Festival); The Woods (Company of Angels) and Romeo and Juliet (OUDS Thelma Holt Japan Tour).

Film includes: Chances (Post Production) and Schwanger (German Lang).

Radio includes: BBC Carleton Hobbs Prize.

Creative Team Biographies

Timberlake Wertenbaker Writer

Timberlake grew up in the Basque Country and lives in London. She has been Arts Council writer in residence with Shared Experience and the Thames Television writer in residence at the Royal Court. She was the Royden B Davis visiting professor of drama at Georgetown University, Washington DC, 2005-2006, the Leverhulme Artist in Residence at the Freud Museum in 2011 and is currently Chair in Playwriting at the University of East Anglia. She is the recipient of numerous awards including an Olivier award and the New York Drama Critics' award for Our Country's Good, the Writers' Guild, Critics' Circle and Susan Smith Blackburn awards for Three Birds Alighting on a Field and the Eileen Anderson Central TV Drama Award for The Love of the Nightingale.

Productions include: The Ant and the Cicada (Royal Shakespeare Company); Our Ajax (Southwark Playhouse); The Line (Arcola); Galileo's Daughter (Bath Theatre Royal); Credible Witness, The Break of the Day, Three Birds Alighting on a Field, Our Country's Good, The Grace of Mary Traverse, Abel's Sister (Royal Court); The Ash Girl (Birmingham Rep); After Darwin (Hampstead Theatre) and The Love of the Nightingale (Royal Shakespeare Company).

Translations and adaptations include: Racine's Britannicus (Wilton's Music Hall) and Phèdre (Stratford Shakespeare Festival, Ontario); Euripides' Hippolytus (Riverside Studios) and Hecuba (ACT, San Francisco); Sophocles' Theban Plays (Royal Shakespeare Company) and Elektra (ACT, San Francisco); Jean Anouilh's Wild Orchids (Chichester Festival Theatre); Eduardo de Filippo's Filumena (Peter Hall Company at the Picadilly) Gabriela's Preissova's Jenufa (Arcola); Ariane Mnouchkine's Mephisto (Royal Shakespeare Company) and Marivaux's False Admissions and Successful Strategies (Shared Experience at the Lyric Hammersmith).

TV and Film productions include: The Children and Do Not Disturb.

Opera includes: The Love of the Nightingale, music by Richard Mills (Perth International Arts Festival and Sydney Opera House).

Radio includes: Dianeira; What is the custom of your grief?; The Memory of Gold; an adaptation of A. S. Byatt's Possession and, most recently, a ten hour dramatization of Tolstoy's War and Peace (Jan 1, 2015).

Timberlake also wrote Isaac Newton's phone call for Talking Statues (British Library Courtyard).

Brigid Larmour Director

Brigid is Artistic Director and Chief Executive of Watford Palace Theatre. Productions directed for the Palace include: Love Me Do (co-directed) and Von Ribbentrop's Watch by Laurence Marks and Maurice Gran; Gary Owen's Perfect Match (part of the Ideal World season), We That Are Left and Mrs Reynolds and the Ruffian; Ronald Harwood's Equally Divided; Charlotte Keatley's Our Father and My Mother Said I Never Should; Alan Ayckbourn's Time of My Life and Absent Friends; Shakespeare's As You Like It; and pantomimes Mother Goose, Robin Hood and Sleeping Beauty (co-directed) by Andrew Pollard.

Brigid is a producer, director, dramaturg and teacher with experience in the subsidised and commercial theatre and television. From 1998 to 2006 she was Artistic Director of West End company Act Productions, and adviser to BBC4 Plays. From 1993 to 1998 she directed a series of promenade Shakespeares, Shakespeare Unplugged, for RNT Education.

From 1989 to 1994 she was Artistic Director of Contact Theatre, Manchester, commissioning the first British plays responding to the rave scene (Excess/XS), and the implications of virtual reality (Strange Attractors, a multimedia promenade production, by Manchester poet Kevin Fegan). She trained at the RSC, and as a studio director at Granada TV.

James Button Designer

James studied at Wimbledon School of Art. For Watford Palace he has previously designed The Trial, Gulliver's Travel, Grimm Tales and Milestones. Recent designs for theatre include Albion (Bush Theatre); The Nutcracker and the Mouse King, The Velveteen Rabbit, Not Now Bernard, Henry the Fifth, A Winters Tale and Dr Korczak's Example (Unicorn Theatre); Little Shop of Horrors, Worst Wedding Ever and On Golden Pond (Salisbury Playhouse); Macbeth, Tory Boyz, Romeo and Juliet and Prince of Denmark (Ambassador's Theatre); Mad About the Boy (tour); Absent Made Present (Royal Opera House); Johann Strauss Gala (Barbican and Tour); Orpheus and Eurydice and Our Days of Rage (Old Vic Tunnels); Fen (Finborough Theatre); Relish (Tramshed); Rewind and King Lear (Young Vic). Film Credits include: costume design for Watch Over Me (Series 4) and Spiralling. James was also the costume designer for the Welcoming ceremonies of the 2012 Olympic Games and 2014 Commonwealth Games.

Prema Mehta Lighting Designer

Prema graduated from The Guildhall School of Music and Drama.

She has designed the lighting for over one hundred drama and dance productions, including: Fourteen (Watford Palace Theatre); Hercules (New Art Club on tour); The Great Extension (Theatre Royal Stratford East); The Electric Hills (Liverpool Everyman); Dhamaka (O2 Arena) and Maaya (Westminster Hall). She is currently working on the launch of a new figure at Madame Tussauds.

Shona Morris Movement Director

Shona is Head of Movement at Stratford Theatre in Canada.

Shona's recent productions for Watford Palace Theatre as Co-Director include: Sleeping Beauty by Andrew Pollard and the premier performance of Laurence Marks and Maurice Gran's play Love Me Do.

Her recent work as Movement Director includes: King John, A Midsummer Night's Dream, Hayfever, Mother Courage, King Lear (2014), Romeo & Juliet, Blithe Spirit, Waiting for Godot, The Three Musketeers, Mary Stuart (2013), Peter Pan, Dangerous Liaisons, The Winter's Tale (2010) and The Birds, The Flies, Agamemnon, Electra, King Lear, Henry VIII (2004 – 2007) (Stratford Festival Theatre); Perfect Match, Override (2013), Our Father, My Mother Said, As You Like It, Lysistrata, The Dresser and An English Tragedy (2009 – 2012) (Watford Palace Theatre); The Snow Spider (2011) (Io Theatre); Atman (2010) (Finborough Theatre); Swine (2009) (National Theatre Studio); Nicholas Nickleby, Twelfth Night (2005 – 2008) (Chichester Festival Theatre); I Caught Crabs in Walberswick (2007) (Eastern Angles/Edinburgh Festival/Bush Theatre).

Shona's work as an actor includes: Chicken Soup with Barley (Nottingham Playhouse/ Tricycle Theatre); Augustine; Big Hysteria, Wax and Crossfire (Paines Plough).

Shona also teaches at Drama Centre as a mask and movement teacher where she also directs and at RADA where she teaches movement.

Catherine Jayes Musical Director

Musical Director/ Supervisor/ arranger: Calamity Jane (presently on a National Tour from The Watermill Theatre); The History Boys (National Theatre Tour); The Color Purple, Road Show, Torch Song Trilogy (Menier Chocolate Factory); Merrily We Roll Along (Menier Chocolate Factory and Harold Pinter Theatre - winner of Evening Standard Award for Best Musical and Olivier Award for Best Musical Revival); Oklahoma! (Chichester Festival Theatre); Gypsy, High Society, Fiddler on the Roof (West Yorkshire Playhouse); Guys and Dolls, Sweet Charity (Sheffield Crucible); many productions at the Open Air Theatre including: The Pirates of Penzance, Kiss Me Kate, Kate, High Society, The Boys from Syracuse (Olivier Award for Best Musical Production) and The Boy Friend.

As MD/ arranger for actor/musicians: Animal Farm (West Yorkshire Playhouse); Merrily We Roll Along, Irma la Douce, Carmen (Watermill, Newberry); Amadeus (Wilton's Music Hall) and Candide (Liverpool Everyman).

As Composer: An Ideal Husband (Chichester Festival Theatre); Sleeping Beauty, Notes to Future Self, The Cherry Orchard, His Dark Materials, Hapgood, Uncle Vanya (Birmingham Rep); The Mandate (National Theatre, Cottesloe); The Changeling, Macbeth, Cymbeline, The Duchess of Malfi (Cheek by Jowl); The Letter (Wyndham's Theatre); Arcadia (Bristol Old Vic); Great Expectations (RSC); A Midsummer Night's Dream, The Comedy of Errors and The Merry Wives of Windsor (Open Air Theatre).

Films include: Stoker; Charlie and the Chocolate Factory and De-Lovely.

Catherine is an associate director of Cheek by Jowl.

Watford Palace Theatre...

is a 21st century producing theatre, making new work across the art forms of theatre, dance, outdoor arts and digital, and developing audiences, artists and communities through exciting opportunities to participate.

Watford Palace Theatre commissions and produces plays from a range of new and established writers. Recent premieres include Love Me Do by Laurence Marks and Maurice Gran; An Intervention by Mike Bartlett (in co-production with Paines Plough); Shiver by Daniel Kanaber; the Ideal World season of three new plays - Perfect Match by Gary Owen, Virgin by E.V.Crowe (in co-production with nabakov), Override by Stacey Gregg; Jumpers for Goalposts by Tom Wells (in co-production with Paines Plough and Hull Truck Theatre); Our Brother David by Anthony Clark; Our Father by Charlotte Keatley; and Family Business by Julian Mitchell.

Creative Associates are central to Watford Palace Theatre's vision – these include Resident Companies Rifco Arts and Tiata Fahodzi; nabokov; Mahogany Opera Group: Scamp Theatre; Kate Flatt; Shona Morris; Charlotte Keatley; Gary Owen; Stacey Gregg and Alice Birch.

Help Fund our Future

If Watford Palace Theatre and what it represents are important to you, please consider supporting us with a gift in your Will.

Whether you are a supporter of our work on stage, have an interest in engaging young people through theatre, or would simply like to support the Palace as a whole, we hope that you will consider remembering us with a gift in your Will.

Your most personal and lasting gift can be of any size; every donation helps and no amount is too small. By leaving a legacy you will be helping future audiences to discover the wonder of theatre and enjoy Watford Palace as you do today.

Watford Palace's charitable status may offer you the opportunity to reduce the tax due on your estate.

For further information please contact Lynne Misner, Development Manager, on 01923 257472 or alternatively email development@watfordpalacetheatre.co.uk

Thank you for considering this special gesture.

Friends
Support a local theatre with a national reputation

Our Friends receive (£45 per annum)
• Priority Information and Booking
• Discounted tickets (up to 20% on most performances)
• 20% discount on all beverages in our Cafe & Bar
• No card payment, postage or exchange fees

Our Good Friends receive (£90 per annum)
All of the above plus:
• 10% discount on hires of WPT Green Room Bar, Cafe & Hospitality Room
• Private backstage tours for up to 6 guests (normally £20)
• Acknowledgement in show programmes for WPT productions

Our Best & Business Friends receive (£500+ per annum)
• Private backstage tour for up to 12 guests (normally £30)
• Complimentary press night tickets plus drinks
• Opportunities to meet the cast of selected productions
• And more exclusive offers

For Watford Palace Theatre

Supported by
**ARTS COUNCIL
ENGLAND**

www.watfordpalacetheatre.co.uk

Jefferson's Garden

Timberlake Wertenbaker grew up in the Basque Country and lives in London. Her plays include *Our Country's Good*, *The Grace of Mary Traverse*, *Three Birds Alighting on a Field*, *The Break of Day* and *Credible Witness* (for the Royal Court), *The Ant and the Cicada*, *The Love of the Nightingale* (RSC), *Galileo's Daughter* (Theatre Royal, Bath), *The Ash Girl* (Birmingham Rep), *After Darwin* (Hampstead Theatre), *The Line* (Arcola Theatre) and *Our Ajax* (Southwark Playhouse). Her translations and adaptations include Euripides' *Hecuba* (ACT, San Francisco), Eduardo de Filippo's *Filumena* (Piccadilly), Gabriela Preissova's *Jenufa* (Arcola), Sophocles' *Elektra* (Getty), Racine's *Phèdre* (Shakespeare Festival, Stratford, Ontario), Racine's *Britannicus* (Wilton's Music Hall), Ariane Mnouchkine's *Mephisto* and Sophocles' *Theban Plays* (RSC). Opera includes *The Love of the Nightingale*, music by Richard Mills (Perth International Arts Festival and Sydney Opera House). Radio includes *Dianeira*, *The Memory of Gold*, an adaptation of A. S. Byatt's *Possession* and a ten-hour dramatisation of Tolstoy's *War and Peace*. Timberlake is the artistic director of Natural Perspective and Chair in Playwriting at the University of East Anglia.

TIMBERLAKE WERTENBAKER

Jefferson's Garden

FABER & FABER

First published in 2015
by Faber and Faber Limited
74–77 Great Russell Street
London WC1B 3DA

Typeset by Country Setting, Kingsdown, Kent CT14 8ES
Printed and bound by CPI Group (UK) Ltd, Croydon CR0 4YY

A CIP record for this book
is available from the British Library

ISBN 978–0–571–32512–2

2 4 6 8 10 9 7 5 3 1

Jefferson's Garden was first performed at Watford Palace Theatre on 5 February 2015. The cast was as follows:

Christian David Burnett
James Burt Caesar
Daniel / Mason / Perrault Gregory Gudgeon
Jefferson / Carl Christian William Hope
Susannah Mimi Ndiweni
Sally / Betty Carlyss Peer
Harry / Madison Joseph Prowen
Martha / Nelly Rose Julia St John
Louisa / Imogen / Patrick Henry Anna Tierney
Chorus full company

Director Brigid Larmour
Designer James Button
Lighting Designer Prema Mehta
Movement Director Shona Morris
Musical Director Catherine Jayes
Dialect Coach Helen Ashton

Characters

in order of appearance

The Historical Chorus

Carl Christian

Daniel

Martha

Louisa

Imogen

Christian

Harry

Susannah

Mason

Jefferson

James

Patrick Henry

Tory

Nelly Rose

Madison

Patriots

Nash

Sally

Betty

Monsieur Perrault

JEFFERSON'S GARDEN

*This version of the text went to press
while rehearsals were still in progress, and
may differ slightly from the play as performed.*

*In the passages spoken by the Chorus, a bold dash
before a line indicates that a new member
of the Chorus takes up the speech.*

Act One

The Historical Chorus comes on.

Chorus For a long time it was believed that no story could be told without the help of a muse.

— Looking wafty and with not many clothes on, she would breathe life into beginnings.

— Clio was the muse of history, spelled as in the car made by Renault, also the name of the odd cat.

— She was the daughter of Zeus, god of thunderstorms, fireworks and these days, guns. She fell in love with a human being and became the goddess of family, the beginning of all history.

— Then the muses, like much of history, were forgotten, dismissed, considered old-fashioned, sexist, unnecessary, elitist, and foreign.

— But some might tell you that what really happened is that she became internalised and lives on in our collective need to remember.

— Who else can we call on now to help us recreate on this bare and beautiful stage a rebellion?

— Actually, a revolution.

— Insurgency: words shift depending on who's talking.

— Really the story of a family.

— We will take on many roles, sometimes with names, sometimes without.

— Names and no names always interweave in history.

— We have to ask you to be gender-blind, colour-blind, age-blind, shape-blind, but in all other ways perceptive.

— We have some extraordinary language that has been handed down to us like sacred props.

— 'When in the course of human events it becomes necessary for one people to dissolve the political bonds which have connected them with another –'

Chorus (*over*) The call to freedom. Clio means: I call.

Chorus Historical events usually begin with a call.

— And we call on Clio now, who lives in the generosity of your imaginations, to help us –

— – move on to a ship sailing from England to Baltimore, a port in the American Colony of Maryland. We are becalmed, somewhere in the middle of the ocean, in the middle of the eighteenth century and as a chorus of sailors, we have nothing to do but wait – and sing.

Chorus (*sings*)
  Then three times round went our gallant ship.
  And three times 'round' went she
  And the third time that she went 'round'
  She sank to the bottom of the sea . . .

ONE

Carl Christian, Daniel, Martha, Louisa. Carl Christian collapses.

Carl Christian Free. Flowing free from the source . . . *Wasser* . . .

Daniel Try to remain quiet.

Carl Christian Water . . . *Wasser. De l'eau.*

Martha Don't waste our water on him.

Carl Christian Freedom, like water, ran dry.

Louisa He'll die without water.

Martha Dressed like a lord, acts like one and doesn't even have the excuse of being English.

Daniel We have a duty of charity towards everyone.

Martha No one ever showed us charity.

Daniel That was the old world, we are sailing to the new.

Martha We're not sailing anywhere. The ship hasn't moved in days.

Louisa I feel a breeze.

Martha Hope doesn't mean things are there, Louisa.

Carl Christian *De l'eau. Wasser.* Water . . .

Martha Why use different languages if you act the same in all of them? I'll have that water. He's going to die anyway.

Daniel gives Carl Christian water.

Carl Christian I'm dying?

Martha We're all dying on this godforsaken ship. When they promised us land they didn't say anything about all the water in between.

Daniel We were being persecuted.

Martha Persecution is the price of living in England. At least you don't get seasick.

Louisa I still feel the wind.

Martha He has a fever, we could catch it.

Daniel Fear is an agitation of the mind, Martha.

Martha If only this ship would agitate itself a little we might have some hope of this good and free life we were promised.

Carl Christian I too sought this freedom – pursued and agitated, yes, that is the word.

Daniel We do not believe in agitation.

Louisa I feel things before they're there. I feel we are moving. And I feel something about you. What is your name?

Carl Christian Carl Christian Friederich Montbéliard von Württemberg.

They all burst out laughing except for Louisa.

Louisa Why all those names?

Carl Christian To remind me of who I am – to remind others also.

Louisa My name is Louisa. We're from England.

Carl Christian I was not safe there either.

Louisa We've been offered land in America, we'll farm. What will you do?

Carl Christian I left on the first ship. I did not think of arriving.

Louisa There is a new land waiting for us, new hopes and oh, so many possibilities, and we can forget England.

Carl Christian (*smiles*) Can you forget your history?

Louisa Father, you always said we might need someone to help us.

Daniel Can you farm?

Carl Christian I had land.

Martha Worked on by others?

Carl Christian There was too much for one . . .

Daniel In America everyone will have to do things for themselves.

Martha People like him don't do, they are.

Daniel Men are not generalities.

Martha Then why do they act as if they were?

Daniel (*to Carl Christian*) What are you good at?

Carl Christian I ride, I brought my rapier. I can teach fencing? Perhaps dancing? I can teach French. And German of course.

Daniel In America, people only want to learn what is useful. We have carpenters here, we have bakers, cloth-weavers, glassblowers, masons. What can you make?

Carl Christian Make?

Martha My husband is asking, have you ever seen a tool and can you make yourself useful?

Carl Christian The most useful is to give people tools for freedom, no?

Daniel Freedom comes from within.

Carl Christian Within the people – like water. I wished to be useful and show people they do not need to submit. We were betrayed.

Daniel I do not want to hear more.

Louisa Father, Carl Christian Frederick will die without our help.

Martha It sounds like he already ought to have been hanged for rebellion.

Daniel We were rebels too, Martha, in our way. Wouldst thou let a man die? (*To Carl Christian.*) I am a shoemaker. I can teach you my trade. But in exchange you will hand over your rapier and renounce all that it represents. You will agree never to engage in any of your previous activities and to forget all your ideas.

Carl Christian If I forget my ideas, who am I?

Daniel A new country does not need old ideas. Let me see your hands.

Martha How is he going to exchange such soft hands?

Daniel Your hands are weak but that's because they've never been used.

Carl Christian Is it difficult to learn – this use of hands, this 'making?'

Daniel You'll discover a new world.

TWO

Chorus As the historical chorus, we have the freedom to choose the moments we think important. Drama, conflict, all that stuff.

— And the ones we enjoy: we like travel, generally, change.

— But nothing much happens for twenty years. The family settles on a farm in Maryland. Louisa, as you've already guessed, marries the handsome Carl Christian. They have two children, Christian and Imogen. Louisa dies young.

— Imogen is now seventeen and a perfect replica of her mother.. Daniel and Martha have kept their looks and appear exactly the same as in the previous scene, as does

Carl Christian. In this Quaker household, the early evening is devoted to quiet.

Everyone sits, very still and straight. A short silence.

Daniel Today I spoke with a British soldier. He described his memories of the French–Indian wars. He confesses he fought with savagery and partook in torture. He is to return to England soon and I fear it will be as a man broken by violence.

Do mankind, walking in uprightness, delight in each other's happiness? Or do they employ their skill and strength to afflict and destroy one another? Attend then, my soul, to this wisdom: remember the quietude of the heart.

Imogen Grandfather: today as I was working in the house I remembered what thou hast said about inward prayer, how the prayer of the heart is without words, without thoughts. How will I recognise it?

Daniel Thou wilt know it when it comes to thee. It is the unutterable prayer, the fruit of love. Let not thy thoughts disturb it.

Martha I am aware that although I seek peace and quietude in my heart, in my thoughts is the knowledge that the potatoes are overcooking.

Daniel We have always valued the work of our hands but we try to work with quietude in our hearts.

Martha I ask myself, how can I make the potatoes understand this?

Daniel If no one else is moved to speak we will draw this meeting to a close. Carl Christian?

Carl Christian When that soldier spoke to you, he rekindled his memories of violence. Is it not better to remain silent always?

Daniel Words are not treacherous when they come from the quiet heart.

Carl Christian How certain, even after all these years, can I be of the quiet of my heart?

Martha A happy and well-fed family brings quiet to my heart.

Daniel Is it not rather the reverse? We are happy because we are quiet?

Christian bursts in, booted, breathless.

Thou art welcome, Christian. Come, sit thee by me. The meeting is still open if thou art moved to express what is in thine heart.

Christian There is such ferment in the town!

Daniel And what dost thou observe in thine heart?

Christian It's boiling. The King has –

Daniel We do not speak of the King at a gathering of Friends. It disturbs the peace.

Christian But we may be at war!

Daniel 'Things that are subject to exterior sense are to mutation most pretence.'

Christian (*over*) But Grandfather!

Daniel O Lord, breathe the balm of thy coolness over the ferment of desires. I bring this meeting to a close.

The rhythm changes, quite frenetic.

Carl Christian Christian, we do not interrupt our elders when we sit.

Martha (*over*) The potatoes! (*To Daniel.*) The lamb is burned as well.

Daniel There is a time for everything.

Martha The food doesn't know that. Imogen, help me!

Imogen (*to Christian*) What happened in the town?

Christian The King has refused to hear all petitions whether from American or London merchants. Parliament is calling the colonists rebels and accusing them of treason. The town echoes with the cry of 'Liberty!'

Carl Christian Calm yourself before you speak, son. What is this cry of liberty?

Christian We will not accept to remain the slaves of a Parliament thousands of miles away.

Daniel 'We' live in tranquillity here.

Christian Tranquillity is also found in dungeons.

Carl Christian That is from the philosopher Jean-Jacques Rousseau. How is it you are reading Rousseau?

Christian They were reading it out in one of the taverns.

Carl Christian You frequent taverns!

Christian Not to drink, Father, to hear speeches.

Daniel There are many ways to become intoxicated.

Carl Christian You will renounce all taverns.

Christian I will not renounce liberty, because to renounce liberty is to renounce one's duty.

Carl Christian (*precise*) What Rousseau actually says is: to renounce liberty is to surrender the rights of humanity.

Christian It's the same, isn't it?

Carl Christian (*suddenly agitated*) Not at all – because you have not yet defined what humanity is – but these are all ideas.

He goes still and silent.

Imogen I understand the word humanity because I feel part of it.

Martha Humanity is about the family. It's sitting at a meal around a table that makes humanity.

Christian What's happening now in America –

Daniel Local difficulties do not affect us.

Christian But Grandfather, the cause of America is the cause of all of Mankind.

Daniel If that is so, we must pray for peace.

Imogen I always felt we could make a new kind of history here – I sometimes feel things before they happen.

Martha Your mother felt that too and sometimes she was right and sometimes not.

Daniel Let me remind all of you that our practices have always been to seek peace and do only that which tends to the peace of all.

Christian Didn't you come here seeking freedom, Grandfather?

Daniel We came seeking freedom of worship without persecution or prejudice. We have that freedom here.

Imogen But what about the freedom of others? What about the British blockade in Boston?

Christian All because some men threw a few tea chests in the sea dressed up as Indians. Where's the British sense of humour?

Martha They lost the tea: no one has a sense of humour when it comes to profit.

Christian What about the Quartering Act? They're forcing soldiers into every Boston home.

Daniel We have had British soldiers billeted here, they have been most helpful. We must not forget that they have protected us from the French and the Indians.

Christian But to blockade the port of Boston is an act of war.

Imogen They're starving the women and children and we're doing nothing.

Daniel We are drawing up a petition to the King.

Christian Don't you know that nothing flatters vanity or better confirms obstinacy in kings than repeated petitioning?

Carl Christian Who said that?

Christian I don't know, there are pamphlets being read out on every street corner.

Martha (*over*) The mention of royalty always ruins a good meal.

Christian How can I eat when I am not free?

Imogen How can I eat when others are starving?

Christian and Imogen storm out.

THREE

Chorus Teenagers.

— Which is how the British Parliament regards the American colonists.

— The relation that subsists between America and England is one of parent and child. We are seeing ingratitude in the child and we must chastise it.

— The King himself opens Parliament with –

— That's King George the Third.

— A name the Tea Party gives to Obama.

— Why?

— Probably that same arrogant use of long words.

Chorus / King A most daring spirit of resistance and disobedience to the law, still unhappily prevails in the province of the Massachusetts Bay.

Chorus The debates last months, even years. We'll only give you a few sound-bites.

— The first principle of British liberty is that no man shall be taxed but by himself or by his representative – America has no representatives here!

— Look at the state of our country: beggary and distress. The profits of America are two million a year!

— Is it right that America should be protected by this country but not pay for it?

— However – taxation and representation are inseparably united. God has joined them, no British Parliament can separate them.

— Great Britain has, in all cases whatsoever, a right to lay taxes upon the colonies.

— Can this be done but by force? Let us not drive them to despair. The despair of a brave people always turns to courage

— We, the Parliament, agree to send over some troops. But –

— We were promised that on the very appearance of troops in Boston all was to be tranquillity, yet far from subduing the spirit of the people it has had the contrary effect.

— It's all very familiar: send in the troops, that'll calm the rebels, but history shifts the words.

— Whether their present state is that of *rebellion* or a fit and proper *resistance* to unlawful acts of power, I do not determine. This is know: a successful resistance is a *revolution*, not a rebellion

— The words bounce back and forth across the ocean and into our family.

FOUR

Carl Christian and Christian. Christian is holding a boot.

Christian I can't do this.

Carl Christian It's only a mistake: unstitch it here and sew it again.

Christian My hands keeps slipping.

Carl Christian The hands obey the will.

Christian Maybe I don't have the will. Why did you teach me so many things, Father, if I was always to be a shoemaker?

Carl Christian Who said shoemakers had to be stupid? Let me start the new stitching for you.

Christian But how is it you know all about Rousseau? And can recite Schiller? What about the medicine you taught me? Were you always a shoemaker?

Carl Christian Here, follow this line –

Christian You didn't come from England like my grandparents. You never talk about the past. Why did you leave Europe? What were you, Father, over there?

Carl Christian We don't waste time with the past in America.

Christian Why won't you tell me?

Carl Christian I was a hothead like you. Keep your hand steady.

Christian What do you mean by a hothead?

Carl Christian A man whose mind is enflamed by ideas he doesn't understand. Learn to work, it'll ease the fever of your mind.

Carl Christian You've been brought up by Quakers, in quietude, in a spirit of peace and obedience to a higher law. Stay on that path.

Christian I can't do it! I've ruined the boot!

Carl Christian I ruined a lot of good leather myself and Daniel was always patient. Sometimes your mother had to help me in secret. You have good hands, like hers.

Christian I don't want to make shoes while my country suffers under the weight of tyranny.

Carl Christian (*laughs*) Such weighty words. What can you do against tyranny?

Christian What can one do against oppression but rebel and fight?

Carl Christian Quakers do not fight.

Christian I'm not just a Quaker, I belong to a wider community.

Carl Christian You are a Quaker first.

Christian That was your decision, not mine, but as long as I can reason I am my own master.

Carl Christian Daniel would say you can only become your own master through an internal process of the soul.

Christian That's for me to discover. If I hand over my reason to you or to the Quakers how can I assume my full humanity?

Carl Christian Christian: what are you doing now but exchanging one authority for another, one obedience for another, and putting your humanity at the service of people you don't know – like a child wandering through a dangerous forest. Violence has nothing to do with humanity.

Christian It may be a necessary path.

Carl Christian Don't say foolish things!

Christian It's only foolish to the Quakers and to those who hate liberty.

Carl Christian I won't discuss this any more, you'll finish these boots and forget your ideas.

Christian And if I can't?

Carl Christian Will I have to lock you up to save you from yourself?

Christian That would be violence, Father, and the Quakers disown violence.

Carl Christian Finish these boots!

Christian No.

Carl Christian A son obeys his father.

Christian Until he hears a stronger voice. The call of liberty.

Carl Christian That is a word that could make you lose your family, your community, your own heart and your future. Is that what you want?

Pipes and drums.

FIVE

Chorus
    We led fair Freedom hither
    And lo, the desert smiled!
    A paradise of pleasure
    Was opened in the wild!
    Your harvest bold Americans
    No power shall snatch away
    Huzza, huzza, huzza, huzza
    For Free America!

— The delegates are coming!

— Look at those horses, galloping through Philadelphia.

— It's the Virginians, see how splendid they look, the Sultans of the South, the great orators.

— And their slaves in livery, riding behind them.

Christian Who is the tall one who rides so well?

Chorus That's George Washington from the French and Indian wars. He says he's sworn to raise an army himself and will fight the British though no one join him.

Christian And who is that man with the red hair who rides as well as George Washington?

— That's Thomas Jefferson

— It wasn't on the same day, he came months later.

— It's the same historical moment, the same spiritual moment.

— In the rewriting of history, time jumbles.

— Yes, but what about accuracy?

— A historian told me he doesn't mind as long as we all take a bow at the end.

Christian Thomas Jefferson the writer?

Chorus The Virginians are all writers, they're all orators, we're all freedom fighters.

— I'm not! Surely economic sanctions will be enough?

— We've split into opposing opinions as history always does.

— Huzza huzza for free America! Great Britain adieu, no longer shall we honour you!

— Only fools would try to resist the greatest power on Earth and that is Great Britain.

— Freedom has been hunted around the globe. England has given her leave to depart. Europe regards her like a stranger –

— Zealots of anarchy, that's what the delegates are.

— Oh America, receive the fugitive Freedom, for we are the asylum of mankind.

— And we'll dress accordingly. Formal red coats or brown or blue casual wear depending on which side we're on. And some of us in Quaker black.

The Chorus marches off, leaving one: Harry Westcote in uniform. Christian stares. Daniel comes on.

Daniel You are Harry Westcote? You are billeted with us. Our farm is modest, as you will, see but you are welcome. You will share your first meal with us. Christian, take Harry's things to his room and I will show him around the farm.

Christian does nothing.

Christian, thou wilt obey me.

Harry keeps his rifle. Daniel and Harry exit.

SIX

Christian, furtive. Imogen sees him.

Imogen Like a thief in the night. You can't.

Christian I have to go before it's too late.

Imogen Talk to them.

Christian How can I? My father refuses to speak. We even have the enemy living right here in our house.

Imogen Harry's a young soldier, he didn't ask to come. You could try talking to him.

Christian And say what? That he should fight for liberty and not against it? Do you think he would understand that?

Imogen He's homesick.

Christian Let him go home and leave us in peace.

Imogen We are at peace.

Christian I have to go, Imogen. Freedom is a call and I can't resist it –

Imogen This is your family: ask for their blessing. Or at least their forgiveness.

Christian You know they'll stop me.

Imogen And you steal the horse as well?

Christian I'll bring it back.

Imogen When?

Christian When we have freed this land. Don't you want that too?

Imogen Yes, I want that – but what will you do?

Christian Whatever I have to.

Imogen You can't fight: it's against Quaker rules to fight.

Christian No one is fighting yet.

Imogen Swear that you will never take up arms and that you won't spill blood.

Christian Swearing is against the rules, Imogen, you know that.

Imogen Then you will affirm and declare in the presence of God.

Christian I couldn't live with a broken promise.

Imogen Repeat: I, Christian, do declare –

Christian It's getting light, let me go!

Imogen – in the Presence of Almighty God the Witness of the Truth of what I say and I – Repeat!

Christian I, Christian do declare – I can't.

Imogen I hear them stirring in the house. Stand still. Repeat: I do solemnly, sincerely and truly declare and affirm that I will not spill blood – I'm waiting. I think I hear Father –

Christian I declare and affirm that I will not spill blood. Now let me go!

Imogen Go in peace: you're free.

Christian rushes off.

SEVEN

Imogen, Daniel, Martha, Carl Christian and then the Chorus as Quakers.

Carl Christian Please do not ask me to disown my own son.

Daniel The rules were established by men and women who know that the soul needs its own military discipline to keep peace.

Martha What peace? This family is at war, canst thou not see that, Daniel?

Carl Christian I'm Christian's father and I didn't guide him – or even tell him what he needed to know. The fault is mine.

Imogen Christian only wants to defend the freedom of the land he loves.

Daniel Our land is our community.

Martha What kind of community breaks up a family?

Daniel When we can't find what is right in ourselves, our community is there to remind us. It is what saves us from doubt.

Martha What's wrong with doubt?

Daniel We must start. The Friends are coming.

Martha Friends?

The Chorus moves on, all in black and surround the family.

Chorus We do not approve of the proceedings of the British ministry, we think them ill-advised, but we do not believe in revolution and we do not believe in war. We do not allow any association in any warlike exercise or being in an engagement where others are slain.

The sheet is handed to Carl Christian.

Carl Christian Christian by birth had a right of membership in our Religious Society but through levity, he hath been seduced and drawn away with the Spirit of the Times so far as to enlist and join the active part of war, leaving his place of abode to that end and having given no opportunity to treat with him on this sorrowful occasion. We –

Carl Christian stops, shakes his head, a silence. All wait.

– we – therefore – agreeable to our ancient practice –

He can't go on.

Daniel – think it is requisite to deny him the right of membership among us. Which I now – which I now – confirm.

Carl Christian Christian: thou art cast out of our society.

Daniel We will now mourn Christian in silence.

A moment, like a funeral. Carl Christian in distress. Then all leave except for Imogen and Harry, putting on his military coat.

EIGHT

Harry The regiment is going to Virginia where they're expecting trouble. I'm leaving tomorrow. I've liked staying here, I admire your family. I'm sorry to hear about your brother but I would never disobey my father.

Imogen Perhaps freedom must sweep everything before it.

Harry The colonists don't want freedom, they simply don't want to pay taxes, that's what my father says.

Imogen They don't want to pay unjust taxes imposed arbitrarily upon them by people thousands of miles away who do not represent them, that's what my brother says.

Harry My older brother died in the French–Indian war. My father believes that was a war that benefited the colonists. It was very expensive and England is now bankrupt and so the colonists must help pay.

Imogen But they ought to be consulted and not ordered to do so.

Harry My father says we must fight these insurgents or chaos will reign. I do not know. I've had nothing but kindness from the colonists. And when it's over, I hope to see your family – and you – again. Do you like Shakespeare?

Imogen My father sometimes quotes us lines.

Harry I have some books and I thought you might enjoy these plays. There is someone called Imogen in one of them. I grew up a few hours' ride from where Shakespeare was born. It's a very beautiful part of England, green, bathed by gentle rivers. I think you would like it. We could read together now.

Imogen I – I have to go in.

Harry My only fear is that one day I will fight against your brother.

Imogen My brother has sworn not to fight.

Harry I would do the same if I could. Imogen . . . please don't hate me because of the colour of my coat.

Imogen (*smiling*) Hatred does not bring peace to the soul.

Harry What about love?

Imogen doesn't answer. The Chorus comes on.

Chorus History has a way of interrupting love stories. Harry will eventually move with his regiment to Virginia but we'll get there before by travelling with Christian.

— You have to imagine the soft rolling hills, the lush green of vegetation, the increasing sweetness of the air and the particular hue of blue in the distance as Christian rides south.

— We've played men and women of the street, Quakers, and even a homesick Harry, but we now have to bring you the words of famous statesmen.

— Not statesmen yet, but people who will become important enough to impose their own memories on events.

— And their own words. Some of these words were actually said and some only written well after the events.

— Does it matter? It is a warm evening in the elegant and thriving town of Williamsburg, Virginia. Christian rides along North England Street, past the imposing Governor's Palace made of red brick. He turns left, up Duke of Gloucester Street, past the weaver's shop, the shoemaker's and the blacksmith's. He can see the House of Burgesses at the end of the street but he tethers his horse next to the silversmith's and walks, with a beating heart, up a few steps to his destination. We're already there.

NINE

The Raleigh Tavern, Williamsburg, Virginia. Christian walks in, talking to Susannah, who is black and speaks with a carefully educated voice.

33

Susannah All the private rooms are gone, sleeping in the public rooms is sevenpence ha'penny, there are seventy folk sleeping here tonight so you'll only get the floor. Supper's at eight-thirty and costs a shilling. There's another tavern across the street.

Christian I want to be here.

Susannah (*teasing*) The King's Arms has better food.

Christian It depends what kind of food you're looking for.

Susannah And the greengage ice cream is better at the Shield's Tavern.

Christian I meant – food for the heart. I heard the Governor had dismissed the House of Burgesses and everyone was meeting here at the Raleigh Tavern.

Susannah Mm-hm.

Christian How can Lord Dunmore dissolve an elected body? Isn't that another example of the tyranny we suffer?

Susannah I guess you're not a Tory then.

Christian I've come to Virginia to hear people speak of Liberty!

Susannah You're not one of those British spies, are you? Mr Southall can smell 'em a mile off. You don't sound like a Virginian.

Christian I'm from Maryland, I'm a shoemaker.

Susannah You don't look like a shoemaker.

Christian I make very good riding boots.

Susannah Well, do you now? You know Virginians, they like to ride and they like to talk.

Christian Will anyone come tonight?

Susannah You'll just have to wait and see, mister.

Christian (*polite*) Call me Christian, please. You're the first person I've spoken to in Virginia.

Susannah If that's so you may call me Susannah.

Christian Susannah, do you think I might be allowed to speak to Mr Jefferson?

Susannah Know what they say? Anyone can speak to Mr Jefferson but no one understands him. There's James Hemings on the stairs, he makes so much more noise than his master.

Christian His master?

Susannah Why, Mr Thomas Jefferson of course.

Thomas Jefferson and James Hemings come on with George Mason. James Hemings is somewhat dandified and Jefferson scruffy.

Mason Tom, you must speak this evening.

Jefferson I prefer writing, George.

Mason There isn't that much difference, is there?

Jefferson When I write I can be subtle and balance ideas. Speech oversimplifies. Let Patrick speak.

Mason That's just it: Patrick Henry will get carried away by his own rhetoric and before we know it we'll have declared war on Great Britain.

Jefferson I believe we'll come to that sooner or later.

Mason We must show ourselves men of reason and exhaust all avenues to peace. (*Notices Christian.*) By the way, Tom, I had a letter from our dear friend Nelly Rose Madison. She wants me to look after her son James who's just come down from Princeton. Are you James Madison?

Christian No, but I've come to Virginia to – to –

Jefferson (*to Mason*) What's wrong with William and Mary College here? No Southern gentleman should study up North, they become puritanical.

Mason Tom, we can't allow the British to think this is merely about us not wanting to pay taxes.

Jefferson Why not? Unjust taxes ought always to lead to revolution.

Mason Any step towards independence must be justified by something general, universal even. You could start with something about all men, something like – they are by nature equally free and independent, you'll phrase it better, perhaps with more philosophy.

Jefferson We must appeal to the truth.

Mason Quite. I like the appeal to the truth. But what is it?

Jefferson We could say that there's *a self-evident truth* that all men are created equal – and are endowed by their Creator –

Mason Should we bring God into this? It could make us look irrational.

Jefferson We're not saying God exactly: creation is a metaphor. And from it derive –

Mason – rights –

Jefferson – inherent and inalienable rights – like life, liberty –

Mason Happiness and safety.

Jefferson Happiness is a good political concept. The English like to dwell on misery, this will mark us as different, hopeful, as American.

Mason You see, no one can explain this better than you. You'll say all this tonight, won't you, Tom?

Jefferson I'm not a public man, George.

Mason That remains to be seen. I wonder if that's James Madison –

He goes out. Thomas Jefferson remains, pensive. Christian goes to him.

Christian (*to Jefferson, breathless*) It would be an inspiration, sir, if you spoke. I came to Virginia to understand liberty but for me it was a call of the heart. However, I would want to understand it from first principles, with my reason, because it is reason that makes me human, that is, according to Rousseau . . .

Jefferson (*amused and courteous*) My inspiration has come more from the Scottish philosophers but I admire the French, although they are, perhaps, less practical.

Christian I read your *Summary View of the Rights of British America* in Philadelphia. I particularly liked it when you reminded the King that we were asking for rights not favours and called him no more than a chief officer.

Jefferson That was perhaps a little strong – our dispute is as much with the British Parliament as with the King.

Christian (*quickly*) As you say: bodies of men are also susceptible to the spirit of tyranny.

Jefferson Did you say you were from Philadelphia?

Christian Maryland. I'm a shoemaker – but I studied medicine with my father. I speak French and German. I came to Virginia because – in the hope of – hearing you. I seek liberty, its definition, its meaning, its power. I believe you are the only one who can show us the way.

Jefferson To where?

Christian To freedom, Mr Jefferson. Will you speak tonight? Will you?

Jefferson Perhaps I will. I suppose I can always quote from my pamphlet.

Jefferson leaves. Susannah and James stay.

Christian Did you see that, Susannah? I spoke to him! I spoke to Thomas Jefferson! He's so polite, he's such a gentleman, he looks so noble. And what he said about liberty, about it being inalienable. Inalienable is such a beautiful word: what can't be rightfully taken away, ever.

James (*intones*) Liberty is the greatest temporal good with which you can be blest.

Christian Yes, yes, is that from Mr Thomas Jefferson too?

James And slavery is the greatest, and consequently most to be dreaded, of all temporal calamities.

Susannah James, we've heard all this before. It changes nothing.

James Would you desire the preservation of your own liberty? As the first step let the oppressed African be liberated.

Christian I agree freedom will be at risk until we all have it. Did you write that?

James looks at Christian for a moment and leaves.

Susannah He reads too much and being with Mr Jefferson all the time doesn't help. He acts very superior because he's the son of Mr Jefferson's father-in-law and he got some education.

Christian You mean he's Mr Jefferson's half-brother by marriage?

Susannah That's right, and he's always talking about freedom.

Christian With Mr Jefferson?

Susannah With himself, mostly.

Christian And with you?

Susannah Mm-hm . . .

Christian Who was the gentleman with Mr Jefferson?

Susannah Mr George Mason, he owns Gunston Hall, he's a kind gentleman, interested in trees. Good friends with Mr Nicholas Carter who opened the school for slaves here – that's where I went. Carter's the richest man around here.

Christian You know a lot about these men.

Susannah Well, Virginia's one big family.

Christian Were you born in Williamsburg, Susannah?

Susannah My mother was sold on the steps of this tavern by Mr Jefferson's wife's father to Master Southall, who owns it.

TEN

The Chorus comes on.

Chorus I just love being a Southern gentleman.

— The elegance, the Anglo-southern drawl, the wealth, the horses.

— The formulation of freedom, the passion, the rhetoric, the patriotic fervour, the hope. Oh, it's good to be a Chorus at this historical moment.

Jefferson Can any one reason be assigned why 160,000 electors in the island of Great Britain now give law to four million in the states of America – every individual of whom is equal to every individual of them in virtue, in understanding and in bodily strength?

— This appeal to Roman virtues.

— And superior numbers.

Jefferson Were this to be admitted, instead of being a free people as we have supposed we should suddenly be found the slaves of not one but 160,000 tyrants.

Chorus Freedom, tyranny and slavery all in one sentence but it's too subtle: if we're going rouse ourselves and you to revolutionary fervour, we need more.

Chorus / Patrick Henry Let me: Patrick Henry. The power over the people of America now claimed by the British House of Commons in whose election we have no share –

Chorus Yes, that's good: they tell us what to do but they don't represent us.

— Please don't interrupt Patrick Henry: it's not about the content but like all rhetoric, the rhythm.

Patrick Henry On whose determination we can have no influence, who have separate interests to ours, who are removed from the tenderness and compassion arising from personal connections, must, if continued, establish the most grievous and intolerable species of tyranny and oppression ever inflicted upon mankind...

Chorus That's oratory! A tax problem becomes the liberation of man.

— It's a bit more: it's about who makes the laws –

— Actually Patrick Henry may not even have written this, let alone said it.

— Who cares for the facts? This is an historical drama.

— But if we all agree, there's no conflict.

— We don't: there are a few Tory voices. Otherwise known as loyalists or Royalists.

— Who wants to be a Royalist in this crowd?

Tory I'll do it because our patriotic duty is to obey: I propose we offer an olive branch and make a last attempt to reason with the King.

Chorus It's loyal but it lacks rhythm. That's Tories for you.

Patrick Henry We have remonstrated, we have supplicated, we have prostrated ourselves before the throne and we have been spurned with contempt from the foot of that throne.

Tory Let us avoid the terrible cost of war.

Patrick Henry Is life so dear or peace so sweet as to be purchased at the price of chains and slavery? Forbid it, Almighty God.

Chorus The call to God always works, it means God's been brought on side.

Tory I will not hear speak of independence!

Patrick Henry You may take the course you choose: but as for me, give me liberty or give me death!

Chorus To arms! To arms!

Tory Traitors! Rebels! Terrorists!

Chorus No, that word didn't come in until the French Revolution fifteen years later.

Tory Insurgents!

Chorus No. We're freedom fighters! We're the true Patriots!

— There's a word that shifts about.

— Give me liberty or give me death!

Chorus (*all sing*)
Come, join hand in hand, brave Americans all!
And rouse your bold hearts at fair Liberty's call.

ELEVEN

Early morning after a late night. Susannah is cleaning up and Christian comes on.

Christian Susannah, will you bring me a coffee? I believe I've found a way to become the most useful man in Virginia.

Susannah You going to join Mr Patrick Henry's militia? He's been marching outside the tavern all morning.

Christian I promised my sister I wouldn't fight.

Susannah How can you call yourself a Patriot if you won't fight?

Christian You don't need a gun to be a patriot. You know what an English general once said when asked what a soldier needed most in battle?

Susannah No, but you're gonna tell me.

Christian He said what a soldier needed first was a good serviceable pair of shoes, second another serviceable pair of shoes and third, a pair of half-soles. Mr Jefferson has asked me to make a pair of boots for him. I think it's only because he wants to help me stay in Virginia.

Susannah You love that Mr Jefferson, don't you?

Christian There is no one I like listening to more, except my sister and you, with all your knowledge of Virginia. You'd like my sister – do you have a sister?

42

Susannah How would I know?

Christian Doesn't Mr Southall have another daughter?
A little one?

Susannah She'll be my mistress one day, not my sister.

Jefferson and Mason come in.

Jefferson It seems that last night Patrick Henry gave the
first impulse to the ball of revolution, but George, we
can't base a revolution on a slogan which has two 'me's
in it. 'Give me liberty or give me death.' Where is the
definition of liberty? Where are the first principles of
government? The universal equality of man?

Mason We will make sure you write these, Tom, but
even you love the word liberty.

Jefferson Not as an emotion, or even a fact, but as a
concept.

Christian *(timid)* Mr Jefferson, I keep thinking about
what you said yesterday about the inalienable right to
liberty.

Jefferson *(to Mason)* Tyrannies are shaped by the power
of armies but we must have a country shaped by the
power of words.

Mason We're counting on you to do just that, Tom.

Christian *(to Jefferson, timid)* May I measure you for
your boots?

Mason There was some disturbance in the town last
night, did you hear it?

Jefferson I've heard our Governor is about to make a
proclamation, I've sent James out to hear it. He should
be back.

Jefferson sits and is measured.

Christian (*to Jefferson*) I need the height of the calf from the bottom of the heel – now round the middle of the foot – exactly across the joint. It's very useful to know anatomy when measuring for boots. Sir, what did you mean when you said happiness was a political concept?

Nelly Rose and James Madison sweep in, Madison in the wake of Nelly Rose.

Nelly Rose Dear George, what a trip we've had. All we hear is talk of revolution and why *is* Patrick Henry marching up and down out there? He hardly had the courtesy to greet us but then he was always a ne'er-do-well – stay away from him, Jim, the man can't farm, went bankrupt, almost ruined the family and killed his poor mother with worry, and now he thinks just because he took the bar in six weeks he can run the revolution. Tom, how is dear Martha? I haven't seen her since you've hidden her away in that mountaintop of yours. She was always such a delicate creature but such a good dancer. (*She spots Christian.*) And who are you, young man? Have you travelled from the North like my son? And now I must introduce Jim. He's just come down from Princeton but it's taken us a long time to get here because Jim would stop and ask everyone what was going on, he calls it studying the mood of the place, well, it doesn't take a lot of conversation to know the mood of Virginia, you can pick it up by just feeling, but he's been in Princeton and doesn't understand feeling. Well, Jim, what did you find out?

Madison (*after greetings*) I've just been told that the Governor Lord Dunmore filled a wagon with all the gunpowder of Williamsburg and sent it out of town, covered, with a detachment of soldiers in the early hours of the morning.

Nelly Rose Well, I would have done the same thing to keep you men from blowing the whole town up, it's such a pretty town too, so much improved since I was here last.

Jefferson That gunpowder belongs to the town of Williamsburg. It is a deliberate provocation.

Nelly Rose And his predecessor was so charming, I remember the dances he gave.

Christian If Lord Dunmore has confiscated the gunpowder of the town, that is an act of tyranny.

Madison It is probably illegal but I wouldn't call it tyranny. Has a petition been drawn up?

Christian Nothing flatters or better confirms obstinacy in kings more than repeated petitioning.

Jefferson Well thought, Christian.

Christian I didn't think it myself, I read it in a pamphlet by Tom Paine.

Jefferson It doesn't matter who says what as long as it's well said. I'm always repeating George's words here.

Madison I don't think much of Tom Paine, he's too sentimental.

Nelly Rose Jim has such a cool head, and when there's a war no one will be more calm and thoughtful. I suppose we do have to go to war?

Jefferson A self-important man representing a country in the wrong is a fatal combination. Boston is already in revolt and if Dunmore provokes Virginia to revolt as well –

Mason We have to hope he'll be reasonable.

Jefferson In my experience when an Englishman feels his social authority is being questioned he becomes totally unreasonable.

Madison I heard Lord Dunmore was from Scotland.

Jefferson Sadly, in his case, it's made him all the more English. Christian, have you finished?

Christian I need a last measurement.

Madison (*to Christian, dismissing him*) Ah – you're a shoemaker.

James Hemings rushes in.

James I heard every word of Lord Dunmore's proclamation.

Jefferson James has the best memory of anyone I know. Go on James, exactly as you remember it, please.

James (*acts formal, with a very good imitation of a Scottish accent*) 'An army is now on the march to attack His Majesty's troops.'

Nelly Rose I've come all the way from Montpelier and the only American troops I've seen is Patrick Henry marching up and down the street getting breathless.

James 'In order to defeat such treasonable purposes –'

Mason To question authority is not an act of treason. I don't like it when the meanings of words slip about like dead fish in a boat.

Jefferson The use of the word treason is deliberate and will allow the British to hang our people without trial in England. Continue, James.

James 'To defeat such treasonable purposes I do by virtue of the power and authority given to me by His Majesty –'

Christian But isn't that the very power and authority that we are questioning?

James (*exploding*) I can't remember all the words if I'm interrupted all the time.

Jefferson (*calm*) Please continue, James.

James 'And to the end that peace may be restored, I do require every person capable of bearing arms to resort to His Majesty's standard.'

Mason He won't get many volunteers!

James 'And I do hereby further declare all indented servants, Negroes and others, free – that are able and willing to bear arms, they joining His Majesty's troops –'

Jefferson I must stop you there, James, repeat that.

James 'And I do hereby further declare all indented servants, Negroes and others, free – that are able and willing to bear arms, they joining His Majesty's troops.'

Mason He is offering freedom to our slaves if they escape, fight against us and kill us.

Nelly Rose What a silly little man, but then his manners were never very good.

Christian (*gently*) But surely the notion of freedom must appeal to all?

Jefferson We asked Britain again and again to stop the slave trade. The King refused. He's the one who forced this grim commerce on us. And now, with his majestic English logic, he wishes to pay off his own crimes against liberty by urging them to commit crimes against all of us who are fighting for liberty.

Mason How many slaves will be lured by these words into escaping?

Susannah and James remain expressionless.

Jefferson We're one big family in this colony.

Mason I would propose that those who do be granted immediate pardon if caught.

Jefferson I would find it hard to forgive anyone who chose to fight against our noble cause of liberty.

Madison We have laws. Runaway slaves are always punished by law.

Christian (*timid*) But these are laws handed down from the British.

Madison Laws must be obeyed until legally challenged by lawyers.

Christian Even if they go against a man's right to freedom?

Nelly Rose (*to Christian*) What part of Virginia did you say you were from, young man?

Jefferson (*to James*) Where is Lord Dunmore now?

James (*in his own voice*) They say he's gone south to the port of Norfolk.

Mason Norfolk is a nest of Tories, they'll rally round the King's standard.

Jefferson Let the Tories rally around the King: our standard is liberty and we must defend it.

Madison I shall return to Montpelier tonight and raise a militia.

Nelly Rose Jim, your constitution is too delicate to go to Norfolk, there are too many swamps. You can help Tom Jefferson think.

Jefferson (*to James Hemings*) We'll ride to Monticello tonight. (*To all.*) We are now actors on a most conspicuous stage which is designed by providence to display human greatness. It's George Washington who said something like that but I think I've made it sound better.

Christian Mr Jefferson, your boots?

Jefferson The boots will have to wait. I suppose you'll join a militia? Come and find me when America is free.

All leave. The Chorus comes on, singing.

TWELVE

Chorus
No tyrannous acts shall suppress your just claim,
Or stain with dishonour America's name.

— Carried away by the cry of liberty, we leave our shops, our farms and join the militias moving south from Williamsburg towards Norfolk, fifty miles away.

— We move past deserted and pillaged plantations.

— We've been told that Dunmore has moved his troops ten miles south of Norfolk to the town of Great Bridge on the southern branch of the Elizabeth River.

— Where? Anyone have a map?

— We move quietly and reach Great Bridge, once a thriving market town.

— Come close and you see abandoned barges, the water laps unmanned boats, the town stands deserted.

— That heavy hush of war.

— Dunmore has erected a fort on the north side of the river. And look there: four cannons cover the bridge.

— We quietly take positions on the other side of the bridge.

— Dunmore thinks he's going to have the advantage of a surprise attack.

— But we, the Patriots, are waiting.

Christian comes on sewing a boot, followed by a hobbling Patriot. The others place themselves in positions of lookout.

Patriot One Something's happening out there. Give me my boot.

Christian If I don't sew it well, the mud'll come in.

Patriot Three Over there: the British are burning the houses. They're wheeling the cannon on to the bridge! The Grenadiers are approaching.

Patriot One What are we waiting for?

Patriot Two Orders from the Lieutenant: hold fire. Let them come close.

Patriot Three What do you call an Englishman who can think straight?

Patriot Four An American.

Patriot Three They're getting closer – look at those grenadiers, six abreast, in perfect parade formation. That's the British for you, they sure know how to march!

Patriot Three There's at least five hundred of them.

Patriot One I could start picking them off now!

Patriot Four What the hell are we waiting for?

A shout offstage:

Nash (*offstage*) Open fire!

All take positions and start shooting through the openings. Except for Christian.

Patriot Three One down!

Patriot Two I count fourteen!

Patriot One Here, Christian, reload my rifle, I'll use my pistol.

Christian doesn't.

Patriot Three The Grenadiers have stopped. They're still in perfect formation. They're wavering in perfect formation. They're going to turn tail in perfect formation!

Nash, a Patriot, runs in.

Nash Hey, Christian sew up my hand, I've been shot.

Christian Where's the doctor?

Nash Shooting – and drunk, you'll do it better.

Christian I need to ask permission.

Nash Hey, you're a free American, we don't ask permission from nobody. Hurry, I'm not telling my grandchildren I sat out the battle of Great Bridge!

Christian begins to clean Nash's hand.

Patriot Three They're wheeling the cannon away! They're turning back!

Patriot One Pretending to turn back is a Grenadier trick, keep shooting!

Patriot Three They're running away. We've won! We've won!

Chorus (*sings*)
   And all the world shall know
   Americans are free

Patriot Four There's at least a hundred dead and wounded out there. Orders are to bring them here, look after them.

Patriots bring in a wounded man on a makeshift plank or blanket.

Patriot Two All yours.

Christian I'm not a professional doctor.

Patriot One We're not professional soldiers but we've won the battle of Great Bridge in twenty minutes!

Patriot Three Tell you what, I'll put him out of his misery.

He aims a pistol, is about to shoot.

Christian Bring him over here!

They do, bouncing the wounded man.

Patriots (*sing*)
Yankee Doodle went to town –

Whoopsie Daisy—

A black soldier limps on, bleeding badly. The men drop the soldier and stare.

Patriot One Cock-a-doodle-doo: what have we here?

Patriot Three A living member of the Royal Ethiopian Regiment. Just look at what's sewn on here: Liberty to Slaves. Well now, we can get rid of that.

The Patriot slices the jacket. The slave is female.

Patriot One Well, I'll be a Mississippi snapping turtle –

Patriot Two A female Ethiopian.

Patriot Three What we going to do with that?

Christian She's wounded in the leg.

Patriot One kicks both legs.

Patriot One Which leg?

The slave crumples.

Christian Orders are to treat all wounded soldiers.

Patriot Two This ain't no soldier, Patriot, this is a yellow-bellied slider trying to sneak up on us –

He crushes a hand.

Patriot One Let's have all the clothes off –

Christian I won't have this.

Patriot Two You a nigger-lover, Doc?

Patriot Three Fact is, she's someone's property. You damage her, you pay for her, that's the law.

Patriot One We're Patriots, we make the laws now.

A Patriot rushes in.

Patriot Four Orders to collect all the wounded still out there and bring them here fast. We're marching to Norfolk tonight.

All rush out except for Christian. He goes to the slave, who has fainted. He gives her some whiskey from the flask.

Christian Drink this quickly.

Susannah (*shouts*) Give me liberty or give me death, liberty or death!

Christian Shh. They'll hear, why did you leave Williamsburg?

Susannah Things bad in Williamsburg, Master.

Christian It's Christian. Don't you know me? I recognised you immediately – what happened?

Susannah Things bad, ah know what ah knows, Master.

Christian Why are you talking like that? Here, drink some more!

Susannah How'dah talkin'? Like dem slaves?

Christian Why did you leave the Raleigh Tavern?

Susannah Business bad and Master Southall say he was gonna sell his slaves to a man from Georgia – you know about Georgia? The cotton fields of Georgia? That's a quick death and I figure I'd try liberty before death.

Christian Mr Southall wouldn't sell you, he's your father.

Susannah You think that matters to a white man? There was a group making their way to Norfolk to join Lord Dunmore and we talked and sang of freedom the whole way. I never talked to field slaves before, they strong and some of the women decided to join the men and fight.

Christian You're very brave.

Susannah Ain't hard to be brave when there's nothin' to lose.

Christian I've got to get you out of here before it's too late.

Susannah (*sings*)
   Oh freedom, oh freedom
   And before I'd be a slave
   I'd be buried in a grave
   And go home to my Lord and be free!

Christian You'll limp, but you can make your way back to Williamsburg.

Susannah No way, I'm gonna be sold to a man from Georgia. Better die in Virginia than live in Georgia.

Christian If you stay here, they'll rape you, torture you and then lynch you.

Susannah What you think they gonna do in Georgia?

Christian You could go to Mr Jefferson.

Susannah Mr Jefferson? When his slaves don't do what he says he sends them to Georgia.

Christian Could you make your way to Maryland? I can write a letter and say you're my slave. Then you can go to my family.

Susannah I ain't gonna be nobody's slave, Christian, not even yours.

   (*Sings.*) And before I'd be a slave,
   I'd be buried in a grave –

Christian It's only a word.

Susannah Thought you was fighting for a word: freedom. Except you said you wasn't fighting.

Christian I'm not, I'm repairing boots and some feet. Here, you can wear this and you'll look like one of our slaves – no one will notice –

Susannah (*sings*)
   And before I'd be a slave,
   I'd be buried . . .

Christian Everything will change when we've won the war. I know it will. Hurry, they're coming. Get up! You don't get freedom by lying down and singing.

Susannah Maybe that's the only way you do.

She limps out, pushed on by Christian. Patriots come in with another wounded.

Patriot One Some Patriots are staying behind to keep Great Bridge safe, we're marching to Norfolk. Where's that slave? Colonel Woodford wants to question her.

Christian Maybe she crawled out to die. I'm busy.

Patriot One stares at Christian.

Patriot One You didn't let her go, did you, Patriot?

Christian I've been ordered to look after the wounded.

Patriot Two Where's your rifle, Patriot?

Christian I'm a shoemaker. I don't know how to shoot.

Patriot One I'm a weaver, I'll teach you.

Christian I don't have a rifle.

Patriot Two A British corpse gave me his. I'll give you mine. Take it.

Christian I don't need to.

Patriot One Free Americans bear arms.

Patriot Four Leave him alone, if he gets used to shooting he'll be as useless as the doc.

Patriot One Take the rifle. You a coward?

Christian I made a promise – to my sister – my word of honour –

Patriot Two We all make promises to women, it's just words.

Christian We're fighting for a word.

Patriot One Freedom ain't a word: it's a red-blooded American right and we're fighting for it.

The Patriots surround Christian and force the rifle into his hands.

We'll start with a real easy target. One that don't move. See that man over there? That's a British Grenadier.

Christian That's a wounded man.

Patriot One That's why he don't move. We call that an easy target. And he ain't a man, he's an enemy. Got it? Now you hold the rifle like this. You aim. You shoot.

They guide Christian's hands, the shot goes off. The British Grenadier is hit. Christian staggers back, holding the rifle.

Patriot One That's how you get Freedom, Patriot.

End of Act One.

Act Two

ONE

Chorus While you've been enjoying your interval drinks, we've been enduring years of a grim war.

— Both armies are a shambles.

— It was one thing to cry Liberty, join a militia and engage in a few skirmishes but it's another thing to be a soldier under the command of George Washington who can't win a single battle and keeps retreating.

— We're hungry, we're cold. It's snowing. We die by the thousands, and thousands of us simply vanish.

Militia coats off, redcoats on.

— King and country? What are we doing here? Why can't the most powerful army in the world, the British, defeat these badly organised insurgents led by the worst commander in the world, George Washington?

— We pursue this vanishing enemy from New York to Philadelphia, from Philadelphia to Valley Forge, where Washington sets up camp for the winter.

— We're wounded, we're cold, we're lost, we straggle, we vanish. One of us recognises a farmhouse.

A soldier in a muddied and torn redcoat emerges from the Chorus. It is Harry, limping.

Harry Help me! Help!

Imogen (*comes on, calls*) Father!

Harry Don't you remember me?

Carl Christian comes on, sees.

Imogen He's frozen. We have to take him in.

Martha comes on.

Martha We can't take him in. He's a redcoat.

Harry Take off my coat. Remember me? Harry. I gave you Shakespeare.

Carl Christian looks at Harry's hands and feet.

Carl Christian Frostbite. There's no time to lose. (*To Imogen.*) Bring me a bowl of hot water. We must try to prevent the gangrene from setting in.

Imogen goes quickly.

Martha We can't take a British soldier in. The Revolution-aries already suspect us because we won't fight.

Harry I want peace. I'm Harry.

Martha I have to protect the family: you're our enemy.

Harry Only obeyed orders. Times I wondered why we were fighting for swamps and forests, snakes and mosquitoes, and these fanatical insurgents. And then all this snow. It never snows in Shakespeare.

Imogen (*comes on with hot water*) Water . . .

Harry (*to Imogen*) I wanted to walk with you along the river bank, brushing past modest wildflowers, under trees that spread with decorum, the only insects burly humble bees.

Carl Christian This will be painful. We have no brandy.

Harry England – this blessed . . . I can't remember the words. These rebels, they only have one word, liberty, liberty, liberty, and when they kill and they torture, they say liberty. This blessed –

Screams.

Carl Christian The foot is thawing. I need some clean bandages.

Imogen I have them here.

Harry This precious stone. I want to go home.

Carl Christian He must be kept warm.

Martha I cannot let him into the house.

Imogen (*to Martha*) This could be Christian.

Harry I am Christian. No. I remember: your brother is Christian. Alive?

Imogen (*to Martha*) Father and I will carry him into the house.

Martha I won't allow it. I'll save you all despite yourselves. (*To Harry.*) You can't come in, I'm sorry, they'll kill us. It's war. I'll bring you soup. (*To Carl Christian.*) This is the third time you put us in danger to save a soldier's foot.

Carl Christian It will be good for the shoe business.

Martha You think I'm inhuman.

Carl Christian War is inhuman.

Imogen But the light of God dwells in everyone, that's what you taught me, Grandmother.

Martha I love my family. That's the only light I know now.

Imogen He is our greater family. I'm going to save his life.

Martha No, you're not. I'm going to save yours whether you want it or not.

Harry I loved you, Imogen. Thought of you all the years. Did you? . . .

Imogen Yes, Harry, I did.

Harry Take you to England. More beautiful than Liberty. Because so ancient. And small. Plot, that's what it is: 'this blessed plot'. Tell Father, it wasn't worth – There's only life. This earth. Take me in.

Daniel comes on.

Carl Christian The gangrene has set in. He won't last the night.

Daniel Bring him in. Let him die in peace.

Imogen (*to Martha*) I've lost the two men I loved. What is there for me now?

The Chorus with music, pipes and drums.

Chorus And at last, Freedom!

— The British commander Cornwallis surrenders to George Washington in Yorktown on October 19, 1781. Mostly thanks to the French.

— Freedom will always win.

— If you've got weapons and help from a powerful nation.

— Time to take off our redcoats and send them back to England. Bye, King and Country. Of course, later on, we'll miss you and slobber over your princesses.

— We move south once more to the soft hills of Virginia, up to the mountaintop of Monticello. It's quite a climb.

— We're lugging bricks, wood, earth.

— As we climb, we lose our contours. Turn shadowy. We're workers.

— Use the right word, however painful. We're slaves. You might look at us and think, they don't look like slaves but it doesn't matter because –

— We don't count as individuals, although you'll hear us in the background, like water.

— We won't show you any general whippings, chains, blood, rape, wanted posters, because that mostly didn't happen right here in this garden.

— Not today anyway.

— Today we'll sing you a nice slave song.

Chorus (*sings*)
    Wade in the water.
    Wade in the water, children
    Wade in the water
    God's gonna trouble the water.

— But listen to the secret code of History: it's not a nice slave song, it's instructions on how to escape and find freedom:

— You leave no footprints in a river.

TWO

Monticello: Jefferson comes on with James Madison. Jefferson is shabby and limping. James Hemings is also there.

Jefferson The snapdragon, spider flower, cockscomb and love-lies-a-bleeding all survived the British attack on Monticello, as you can see. My reputation did not. Have you heard that Patrick Henry is launching an enquiry into my conduct as Virginia's Governor during the war?

Madison You will be vindicated or my name isn't James Madison.

Jefferson I'm blamed for every Southern defeat. Richmond because I didn't send the militia in soon enough,

Charleston because I didn't predict the enemy would attack from the sea, Camden because it was a general disaster and I had not foreseen this. I'm blamed for escaping from Monticello in order not to end up a prisoner of the British and I'm even blamed for falling off my horse. My public life is over, Jim. I'll continue to build my house and cultivate my garden.

Madison Tom, the real work starts now. We've won the war.

Jefferson No thanks to me –

Madison – but now we have to shape a country.

Jefferson I'll plant tulips here, in this border – and some artichokes, you'd like that, James. (*To Madison.*) James is learning to be a chef.

Christian comes on, with a shiny and beautiful pair of boots. He's been climbing on foot and he's a little breathless.

Christian Mr Jefferson! Hello, James, remember me? Mr Jefferson – don't you recognise me? It's Christian, from the Raleigh Tavern. You said to come and find you after the war.

Madison I remember you: the shoemaker.

Jefferson Christian?

Christian I measured you for a pair of boots. I have them now.

Jefferson I had a bad fall.

Christian I made them of the softest leather. Mr Jefferson, if we're free now, it's because of you and your declaration of independence. I even translated it into French.

Jefferson Did you? But which version? Mine or the one Congress mangled?

Madison It's a great document, Tom, and increasingly seen as such.

Jefferson Did you translate: All men are created equal and independent?

Christian (*quick*) No. I didn't have independent. That would have been better because independent is synonymous with free and it is freedom that ignites the soul. If you omit that, I suppose you imply that not all men have the same right to freedom.

Jefferson Here is a very intelligent young man who understands the virtue of an ideal.

Madison A country composed of as many diverse elements as ours needs to practise the virtue of compromise.

Jefferson Compromise can never be a virtue. A necessity, perhaps . . .

Christian You can never compromise on the question of freedom.

Jefferson (*to Christian*) And when I wrote that all men derived rights, *inherent* and inalienable rights, and these are the *preservation* of liberty, they took out the inherent and they took out the preservation of liberty.

Christian (*very fast*) Yes, I understand: the inherent right to preserve liberty assumes the right to liberty is already there in all men when they are born and therefore any lack of liberty is a violation of that right.

Madison Congress was not made up of young idealists spouting their ideas from the ease of their imagination but of statesmen shaping a momentous decision to go to war. There had to be compromise.

Christian But if America is where the ideal of liberty will be enacted, as on a great stage, as you said, Mr Jefferson, there can be no compromise now.

Madison There will be no liberty at all if this country doesn't survive! This will all be thrashed out in the American Constitution, Tom, and that's why we need you to start writing again.

Jefferson I'll write about the flora and fauna of Virginia.

Christian (*handing the boots to Thomas Jefferson*) Touch this leather. I believe you'll be able to ride in these tomorrow. I also know a way to bandage feet so that they go more easily into the boot. I learned this – during the war. I practised the medicine I knew. I'm hoping to study more.

Jefferson It's a rare thing to be useful during a war.

Christian There were terrible things . . . Mr Jefferson, I have wanted to ask you: the revolution, its violence, were necessary? To gain freedom? And therefore all actions during a revolution are good?

Madison Mr Jefferson has no time for this, we have a new country to worry about.

Christian (*bitter*) Did you fight?

Madison It's not the Revolution but the Constitution that will define America. Tom, you must help write it.

Christian Yes, Mr Jefferson, you would make sure the principles of freedom and equality for all men are enshrined for ever.

Madison You see: even a shoemaker is asking you to write – as well as a lawyer.

Jefferson You're not asking for the same thing and that's the difficulty. Nor are you defining yourselves correctly. You, Jim, are a politician and Christian will be a doctor.

Christian I like making shoes if you think that's more useful in a new country.

Jefferson Shoemaking can be left to the slaves.

Christian But soon there will be no more slaves.

Jefferson Yes, well: Virginia needs doctors and the Constitution needs politicians. But the world needs gardeners.

THREE

They go. The Chorus and James stay. Sally comes on, young and very beautiful.

James Now, Sally, repeat after me:

Sally Did you see the dress Miss Patsy gave me? It has lace here and ribbons.

James Repeat after me: We hold these truths to be self-evident –

Sally I know all that, Brother. Miss Patsy recites it all the time cos it was written by her father: We hold these truths to be self-evident, that all men are created equal, blabby, blabby, blabby.

James Repeat: This idea embraces the Indian and the European, the Savage and the Saint –

Sally That's not how it goes.

James – the white man and the African. You have to learn this by heart, Sally. You're going to go to all the cabins on this mountain to repeat our Declaration of Independence.

Sally We already got one, why'd we need two?

James Mr Jefferson and Mr Madison are talking about a new one, called the Constitution, written down for all

Americans and they must hear us. So now, repeat: Though our faces are black, yet we are men –

Sally My face is almost as white as Miss Patsy's and I'm prettier.

James Therefore let the inherent rights of man be restored . . .

Christian comes on. James immediately stops and freezes and Sally goes still and invisible.

Christian I heard the last words, it sounds good. It's about inherent rights again, and by saying let them be restored, you are saying give back what was stolen. Yes.

James is silent.

James?

James is expressionless.

Do you remember Susannah, who worked at the Raleigh Tavern?

James remains silent.

She ran away, she was wounded and I helped her escape from Great Bridge. I don't know what happened after that. I know you all have ways of communicating. I would like to find her. I only want to know if she's still alive.

A pause.

I thought freedom would be like a mark emblazoned on all of our foreheads, and suddenly, we'd be different men, like a new creation. But freedom seems more like a trickle of water: you scoop it up, it runs through your fingers, and it seems some people must wait their turn to drink.

I am sorry about that.

But I believe this freedom will soon become a river and one day you and I can walk along its embankments. That's the promise of this land, isn't it?

67

I had to do terrible things for that promise. Please tell me where she is. Mr Jefferson wants me to go study with his doctor friend in Philadelphia. I need to know what happened to Susannah.

James (*after a pause*) You'll find Susannah there.

Christian Thank you.

Christian leaves. The Chorus sings softly.

James (*to Sally, more insistent*) Repeat: Therefore let the inherent rights of man be *restored* to the bleeding African.

Sally I'm not a bleedin' African! I'm a beautiful girl and I have a new dress and if I put it on, it won't take much to turn me into a Southern Belle. Watch.

She puts on the dress.

Sally / Betty (*very Southern Belle*) Why, this is the most beautiful garden I have ever seen.

FOUR

Nelly Rose sweeps on, joined by Thomas Jefferson, in mourning.

Nelly Rose My dear Tom, we just had to come and say how sorry we were to hear about your darling wife. She had the sweetest temper this side of the Tidewater but she was always delicate and all that childbirth, well, it just ruins a woman's health, we are so sad for you, aren't we, Betty?

Betty (*very Southern*) Mr Jefferson, I did not have the privilege of meeting your beloved wife but Nelly Rose has never ceased telling me about her and about your garden – and we prayed night and day for God to have mercy . . .

Jefferson It only needed a good doctor to save her.

Nelly Rose Do you think so, Tom? Betty's own mother died giving her birth which is why her father has sent her to us so she can acquire some polish, and she so wanted to see your garden, didn't you, Betty dear? Hasn't Mr Jefferson created the most beautiful garden you've ever seen?

Betty Why, Mr Jefferson, it's divine and those flowers over there are the most beautiful flowers I have ever seen, and they're so – flowery.

Jefferson I have drawn up plans for the west, over there. I only wish the trees near the house would grow faster.

Nelly Rose I'm sure it will be just wonderful but you'll soon be occupied with other things if my son has anything to do with it, where is he? He's always dawdling. I don't know how they put up with him in Congress. Tom, we don't think it's good for you to stay in Monticello when you're so alone and so very sad and mourning Martha, and with all this building around, and who is this very handsome young man carrying books? I've seen you somewhere before, I have such a bad memory unlike my son, now where is that man? I know: Raleigh Tavern, the shoemaker with so many ideas, it was before the Revolution.

Jefferson Christian is about to go to Philadelphia to study medicine with Dr Shippen. I've asked him to concentrate especially on infections in childbirth.

Nelly Rose Betty is very interested in childbirth and tells me she often helped with the slave births and was so upset when so many of them died, well, I hope you'll fix all that, Christian, may I call you that, we're not formal in Virginia but what is your name in case I have to introduce you somewhere?

Christian Christian Friederich von Württemberg.

Nelly Rose Oh dear, that sounds most unfortunately German and even more unfortunately aristocratic, people will think you're one of those dreadful Hessians that awful King George brought over to fight against us. Have you thought of changing it? We like simple names in Virginia, don't we, Tom, nothing too aristocratic, we only believe in the aristocracy of manners, that's very important and of land, too, of course. Tom, I'm so proud of you for stopping that dreadful British habit of giving all the land to the firstborn son, that's not so good for Jim of course but we have plenty to go around and it will mean Betty will have all the land down there, you can see it from here. Christian: you might think of dropping the 'von' that would be an improvement. Here you are at last, Jim, and I'm sure you weren't picking flowers, you were picking your words, now what did you want to say to Tom? I believe there were two things, what were they? I've already said how sorry we were about Martha, you wouldn't know how to convey feeling anyway, Jim, you're a politician.

James comes out and serves iced tea.

Madison Mother believes you ought to get away from Monticello for a while.

Nelly Rose I've already told him that, Jim, why don't you come to the point?

Madison Congress wants to send you to Paris as the American Ambassador.

Jefferson I've left public life, Jim, I'm retired.

Nelly Rose I knew you'd say it the wrong way, Jim. Tom: you speak French, Paris is a beautiful city by all accounts, not that I have any desire to see it, it will change your ideas, and really, being an Ambassador isn't like writing the Declaration of Independence. You only have to be as charming and hospitable as you already are but somewhere else. Is that not so, Jim?

Jefferson I can't leave the girls here, Patsy is only twelve.

Nelly Rose We've thought of all that, you can bring Patsy to Paris with you and she'll get such polish and put all our Southern Belles to shame, even Betty here who is doing so well in that department.

Betty Patsy would be so lucky to learn to speak perfect French.

Nelly Rose Of course Betty already speaks French but the poor thing has no one to practise with. (*To Christian.*) I don't suppose you speak French with a name like that?

Christian I do, Ma'am, my father taught me.

Nelly Rose Then you must speak to my Betty in French.

Madison (*impatient with all this*) We won the war with the help of the French, we owe it to them to send our best man as Ambassador.

Nelly Rose You can take James with you and there's Sally, isn't there? She can look after Patsy. You can't stay here for the rest of your life and look after your garden, Tom.

Jefferson Why not? I would keep writing.

Madison About Virginia?

Jefferson It's like writing about Paradise.

Nelly Rose Jim, have you forgotten that's the second thing you wanted to talk to Tom about?

Madison Could we settle Paris, first, Mother?

Nelly Rose I thought they were entwined. Tom, we both love the notes on the State of Virginia you sent Jim but he would prefer you didn't publish them.

Madison I didn't say that.

Nelly Rose No, of course, you didn't, you're too political to say what you mean, but Tom, you do make the Virginians look bad and that's a terrible thing because of course everyone will want to read anything you write. I'm talking about your chapters on the manners of the Virginians. And here I was telling Christian we have such good manners. By the way, Betty, you wanted to know the names of those plants over there, I'm sure Christian knows them very well, why don't you go and see how many you can name and you can practise your French at the same time.

   Christian and Betty move off.

Don't they make a handsome pair? Do you know anything about his family, Tom? Mind you, we have plenty of family to go around, it's the young men who are scarce, especially the good-looking ones, that always matters to Virginians, that's why we breed such good horses. Now, as I was saying, or as Jim meant to be saying, we can't have you write anything against the Virginians or the Northerners will use it against us and won't let us write the Constitution so that the South can dominate.

Madison Mother, I only said Virginia must lead the way.

Nelly Rose That's what I said. And Tom, you make Virginia sound like such a paradise, except for the slave problem.

Jefferson That's the truth about Virginia, Nelly Rose.

Nelly Rose It's always best to keep truths in the family. Isn't that so, Jim?

Madison I would only ask you to consider a few of your sentences. For example, the one about the unhappy influence on the manners of our people introduced by the existence of slavery.

Nelly Rose We have to show those dreadful British we have better manners than they do. Jim says they haven't even recognised us as an independent country yet.

Madison You say, Tom, that the commerce between master and slave is a perpetual exercise of the most unremitting despotism on the one party and degrading submission on the other. It will not harm the beauty of your book to tone that down.

Jefferson Everything I said and felt about slavery and put in the Declaration was cut by Congress. I could do nothing then. I'm a private man now and I'm free to write what I believe.

Madison But you are no longer a private man, Tom.

Jefferson I didn't say I would go to Paris.

Nelly Rose I know you never like to say anything that binds you, Tom, but of course, you'll go because Jim'll convince you it's important for our country and we only thought you might drop those sentences because you're such a model of courtesy. Now where has Betty gone? Betty! Come here! Your lists of vegetables are so superb and Betty has learned every single one of them, haven't you, Betty? Greens are a good topic of conversation, less vague than landscape. Now Christian, do come and walk with me and tell me about your future studies as a doctor, you must be so clever and Tom of course is a great cultivator of people, he's been wonderful to Jim and I would just love to hear how you came to find yourself in Mr Jefferson's garden.

FIVE

Chorus Think of drops of water.

— A person seeking freedom, alone.

— Finds another drop.

— Soon you have a stream, then a river.

— Made of people. They flow into the streets, gather in small puddles or even a lake. Into a square, a market place, more and more people join in one flow of longing, need and words.

The Chorus takes up stances. Christian comes on, listening and looking for someone.

Chorus (*preacher*) If you love your children, if you love your country, if you love the God of love, clear your hands from slaves.

Chorus The market place fills with the cry of liberty but this is not revolution. The cadences are different, pleading, and hope is thin.

Chorus (*preacher*) We have no property! We have no wives! No children! We have no city! No country! But we have a father in Heaven.

Chorus My brethren, the time is fast approaching when the iron hand of oppression must cease to tyrannise over injured innocence.

— But neither God nor History are there yet.

Susannah comes on.

Christian Susannah!

Susannah (*terrified*) I don't know you!

She tries to get away. Christian holds on to her.

74

Christian Susannah! It's me – Christian – James told me I'd find you in Philadelphia.

Susannah Go away!

Christian Susannah, surely you remember – you were wounded.

Susannah Don't talk about that!

Christian I looked for you as soon as I arrived. Why won't you talk to me?

Susannah I'm a free woman in Philadelphia.

Christian I never questioned your freedom.

Susannah Don't you understand? I'm free as long as I'm here but they send back runaway slaves, it's the law. Go away!

Christian I never stopped thinking of you, all through the war. Then I went to Virginia. Mr Jefferson is helping me become a doctor.

Susannah If you tell anyone in Virginia I'm here, they'll come after me.

Christian I would only tell Mr Jefferson, he's become like a father to me.

Susannah Don't tell Mr Jefferson!

Christian Mr Jefferson is in Paris anyway, with James and Sally, did you know?

Susannah says nothing.

How did you get here?

Susannah We have ways, there's lots of us from Virginia. The Quakers help. I think I've seen your sister, I'm not sure. Have you been back to your family?

Christian The Quakers disowned anyone who joined a militia. I don't exist for them.

Susannah They will forgive.

Christian Not what I did. Not killing. Not murder. The habit of it, the not seeing the human.

Susannah Christian – you saved my life.

Christian Maybe when I become a doctor, when I save a lot of lives, maybe then I can go back.

Susannah Doctors won't treat us, even here.

Christian I'll treat everyone.

Susannah Well, all this talking ain't gonna help me sell vegetables.

Christian Can I see you again?

Susannah You can find me here market days.

Christian Where we could talk quietly, as we did in the Raleigh Tavern – we talked as friends then, didn't we? I loved those times.

Susannah Uh-huh.

Christian Where do you live? Perhaps I could come and find you.

Susannah I don't want to be found!

Christian Please, Susannah, I'm all alone here.

Susannah All right, but don't let anyone see you.

Christian Why not?

Susannah This may be Philadelphia but it's still America.

Christian But we're the ones who are making America.

SIX

Paris. The American Ambassador's house.

Chorus Like travelling salesmen, we seek new markets.

— Don't complain: it's Paris!

— *Liberté, égalité, fraternité.*

— Actually, in 1788, to be precise, it's *liberté, égalité, justice.*

— Somehow, justice will get dropped. Perhaps justice is too complex a notion,

— *Liberté, égalité, fraternité!*

— More catchy. More male.

— Universal brotherhood. Even Jefferson didn't go that far.

— The words inspired by America now flow through the old and narrow streets of Paris and trickle back into the American Embassy.

Monsieur Perrault comes on with James, very elegant.

Perrault Now we are to see the *adjectifs*. An *adjectif* changes, that is modifies, the noun, the thing, it gives it a colour, an interest, so we have the *verbe être* –

James (*very fast and fluent*) *Je suis, tu es, il est.*

Perrault You have an excellent ear, *Monsieur Jacques.* So we have this phrase, *je suis un homme,* I am a man, verb and noun, yes, or in the case of Mademoiselle 'Emings, *je suis une demoiselle*, where is the lovely Mademoiselle Sally 'Emings today? Or you can say about yourself, *je suis un cuisinier.*

James (*irascible*) Not a cook, Monsieur Perrault, *je suis un chef*.

Perrault But now, you want to define your quality, your particularity, yes, so you say *je suis grand* or in the case of Mademoiselle 'Emings, *je suis jolie*, I am pretty, is she not coming today? Ah here is the beautiful Miss Hemings. So now you put the *adjectif* in front of the noun because the *adjectif* is most important and you say *je suis une belle femme*. Like English, I am a beautiful woman, please sit down, *mademoiselle*.

> *Sally is elegant and at ease, Monsieur Perrault bows and generally thinks she's ravishing and stops talking.*

James *Je suis un libre homme.*

Perrault No, in this case the *adjectif* comes after the *nom*.

James That's not right.

Perrault You cannot argue against the rules of French grammar, Monsieur. Let me explain. A beautiful woman is all beautiful, as is Mademoiselle Sally 'Emings, that is what she is, that is her total, no? As you see. But a man is many things, and also free, or busy, or tall.

James (*angry*) No! It is everything. When a man is free, that is what he is, that is his total.

Perrault Monsieur, you pay me and now, *je me rappelle*, you owe me the *leçons* of the last two weeks but you pay me to teach you the *juste* French not the just philosophy, the *adjectif*, as I was saying –

James The words have to be right!

> *Thomas Jefferson comes on.*

Jefferson How is your pupil doing, Monsieur Perrault?

Perrault *Il a un don,* how do you say, he is a gift, *Monsieur l'Ambassadeur,* but he must always remember that although we make good politics with language we make bad language with politics, *n'est-ce-pas?*

He leaves.

Jefferson James, a man must learn always to control his anger.

James Not if he is a French chef.

Jefferson I have a letter from James Madison, they want me back in Virginia. We'll leave next week.

James I don't want to go back to Virginia.

Jefferson I have no choice: Madison wants me to support the new Constitution.

James I have a choice.

Jefferson We'll give a grand farewell dinner, I leave the choice of menu to you.

James When Sally and I stepped on to French soil, we became free, according to the freedom principle established in this country.

Jefferson I know all that, but Monticello is our home. You'll be our French chef there.

James In Monticello, Sally and I are slaves.

Jefferson In Monticello, Sally and you are part of my family, as you are here.

James I want to stay in Paris.

Jefferson I do too, but we can't.

James I can. It's chic to be black in Paris: I'll work in the houses of the nobility. Sally can sew.

Jefferson The nobility is about to be swept away on the tide of revolution.

James Then we'll work for ordinary people.

Jefferson There's no such thing as ordinary people in times of upheaval. Forget all this foolishness.

James It's not foolish to want freedom.

Jefferson Have I ever shown you anything but care and affection? I've put up with your displays of temper because you were part of Martha's family and therefore mine. I've had you trained as a chef, I've paid you a good salary, encouraged you, and all you can say now is that you want to leave my company and my protection and stay in a city that is about to be drowned in civil war?

James I want freedom.

Jefferson You keep repeating that like a parrot screeching a word he's just learned.

James I learned the word from you.

Jefferson Without understanding its complexity, its cost, its myriad and shifting meanings.

James How can I understand all that if I never experience it?

Jefferson Sally, please tell your brother to be reasonable.

James Under French law I'm her next of kin and responsible for her.

Jefferson (*cold*) You seem to have heard a lot about French law but you've neglected a rather important fact: it cost me a considerable sum to have you trained by the best chefs in Paris. In law, you owe me that money. Unless you can pay me back now, I'll have you arrested.

Sally Tom, it's not like you to threaten anyone.

Jefferson Why do you make me do this? You've upset Sally and she shouldn't be upset in her condition. Think what will happen to her if she's alone in Paris.

James She would be with me, a free woman.

Jefferson Free for what? Shall we ask her? Sally, do you want to be left on your own without protection in Paris or come back with me to your home in Monticello. You know I'll never marry again. Think of your child.

James The best for your child is to be free.

Jefferson The best for your child is to be safe.

Sally (*after a moment*) I want to go back to Monticello.

James You'd choose safety over freedom.

Sally I'm choosing what I know.

James (*after a beat*) I'll pay you back as soon as I can.

Jefferson You haven't even paid your tutor.

James Then have me arrested.

Jefferson (*loud*) You'll come back to Virginia with me. In chains if I have to.

James (*shouts*) *Je suis un libre homme – homme libre – homme libre!*

Sally James, remember that Mr Jefferson kept us all together in Monticello when he didn't have to.

Jefferson Listen: come back to Monticello. Train someone else to cook to the standard you've learned here and I will give you your freedom if you still want it. You have my word of honour.

James I want it in writing.

SEVEN

Philadelphia. Susannah, Christian.

Christian Mr Jefferson is asking me to come back to Virginia.

Susannah You want to go back to Virginia?

Christian I want to stay in Philadelphia. I have to do what he asks.

Susannah Are you his slave?

Christian I owe him everything.

Susannah You said we'd go to your family now you're a doctor and have done so much good in Philadelphia.

Christian I'm a doctor because of Mr Jefferson and Mr Jefferson wants me in Monticello. Will you come back to Virginia with me?

Susannah I'm a runaway slave in Virginia.

Christian There are many couples – like us – in Virginia, I used to see them in Richmond, riding openly in carriages.

Susannah You'd have to buy me from my owner, Mr Southall, I'm a young woman of childbearing age, I'm worth a lot.

Christian I know you're worth a lot. (*Pause.*) Mr Jefferson would help us.

Susannah I'd still be your slave, Christian.

Christian Only as far as the law goes – does that matter?

Susannah And then one day you'll find yourself a nice white Southern wife with a plantation and my children will be the slaves of your children.

Christian I'd never do that.

Susannah You haven't lived long in Virginia.

Christian I have to keep my promise to Mr Jefferson.
Please come with me.

Susannah How can I go back to Virginia?

Christian Hasn't it been good here?

Susannah It's been good here.

Christian Hasn't it been good between us?

Susannah It's been good between us.

Christian In all ways?

Susannah Yes, Christian, in all ways.

Christian It might only be for a few years. Couldn't you
bear that?

Susannah Time passes slowly when you're not what
you're supposed to be.

Christian I'm not sure I can live without you, even for a
few years.

Susannah Maybe it's Mr Jefferson you can't live without.

Christian I betrayed my father and everything he taught
me because of Mr Jefferson and his call to freedom. He's
more important to me than my father. I can't betray him
too. I would give up a lot for you.

Susannah But not Mr Jefferson.

Christian That would be like giving up what I have
become.

Susannah Becoming a slave again would be giving up
what I have become.

Christian It's only a word –

Susannah Like freedom? You killed for that word.

Christian I want to be here, loving you, looking after you.

Susannah I don't need looking after. I can look after myself because I know who I am now and I won't let anyone turn me into something else. Not even you.

Christian Will you wait for me?

Susannah No.

Christian When we've had so much in Philadelphia?

Susannah I know Virginia.

Christian You don't seem to know me.

Susannah I do know you.

Christian You don't believe I'll come back.

Susannah I believe you'll come back, Christian.

Christian Then what is it? Don't start one of your proud silences. We'd promised we'd be free with each other.

Susannah I don't know if I'll still be able to love you when you come back.

Christian (*hurt*) I see . . . I'll write.

Susannah Don't.

Christian You want to be free to find someone else.

Susannah I just want to be free.

EIGHT

Monticello. Thomas Jefferson, James Madison, George Mason, Nelly Rose, Betty, Christian. The conversation moves fast, crossing over.

Madison (*to Jefferson*) We need your approval and public support of the Constitution, Tom. George refused to sign at the very last moment and made us Virginians look like fools.

Mason I couldn't sign against my conscience.

Madison A conscience is a private luxury a public man can't afford.

Nelly Rose (*over, to Madison*) My dear Jim, Tom has just come back from Paris and has a lot more to talk about than your Constitution. Christian, I hear you're now a doctor and going to save women's lives.

Christian I have Mr Jefferson to thank for this.

Nelly Rose Let's enjoy Tom's gracious hospitality on this divine summer evening and hear all about Paris.

Madison (*to Jefferson*) I'm sorry but there's so little time, we need your agreement.

Nelly Rose There's always time for good manners, Jim. Christian, do tell Betty about your time in Philadelphia. You must have pined for Virginia.

Christian (*to Betty*) I'm very pleased to see you, Miss Betty.

Madison Mother, I was in Philadelphia too, working through the heat to bind the states together with an American Constitution.

Betty I heard there were many fevers in Philadelphia.

Nelly Rose Now Tom, are the streets of Paris as beautiful as they say?

Mason I hear the streets are awash with the blood of revolutionaries.

Jefferson Yes, but then the tree of liberty must be refreshed from time to time with the blood of patriots and tyrants.

Mason Indeed, it's easy to plant the tree and as you say, blood is plentiful. The difficulty with the tree of liberty is not stunting it before it is fully grown.

Nelly Rose (*to Mason*) I've heard such marvellous things about your cherry trees, George. Betty, Mr Mason has hundreds of cherry trees but he knows how to make them all disappear.

Betty (*to Mason*) Why, that's the most fascinating thing I ever heard, how do you do it, Mr Mason?

Jefferson (*to Mason*) You're not happy with the Constitution?

Madison (*to Jefferson, quickly*) No one can be perfectly happy with a Constitution that brings together the interests of thirteen disparate states, but what about the misery without one?

Mason You can be so determined to get something on paper that you end up with the opposite of what you want. Words twist beyond recognition and liberty suddenly means freedom for the few.

Nelly Rose When you wrote that all men have a right to secure life, liberty and the pursuit of happiness, Tom, you ought to have added – and the right to make very long speeches.

Madison The longer the speeches the less the threat of violence, Mother, that's the point.

Mason As well as to stop us seeing the wood for the trees.

Nelly Rose Isn't that what you do with your cherry trees, George?

Madison (*across to Thomas Jefferson*) We have a constitution.

Nelly Rose Christian, you must know all about constitutions. Jim's is very weak.

Madison I never felt better, Mother, and George was speaking metaphorically.

Nelly Rose Don't metaphor me no metaphors, Jim. Betty, do ask Mr Mason about his trees.

Mason (*to Betty*) If you plant trees in parallel lines, they seem to converge.

Nelly Rose Now there's a metaphor for the Constitution, Jim.

James comes on, very dandified, with drinks.

Why James, you look more Parisian than Tom here.

James The *entrée* will be *asperges sauce blanche* followed by *boeuf bouilli à l'odette de pommes de terre allumettes* and this will be followed by a *Charlotte de fraises sauvages*.

Jefferson It's the custom in France to announce the menu. James insists we keep it.

Nelly Rose Betty, you'll have to translate for me. Weren't you going to practise French with Christian?

Betty (*to Christian*) I hope you will correct all of my mistakes.

Christian I'm certain there will be no need, Miss Betty.

Nelly Rose Now isn't that charmingly said? Jim, you'll never find a wife if all you ever talk about is your Constitution.

Madison (*quickly, to Jefferson*) We scored for democracy by making sure election to the house of representatives would be made by all the people.

Jefferson Excellent. You must approve of that, George?

Mason It depends how you count people.

Madison You count for the purposes of political expediency only.

Jefferson I don't follow.

Nelly Rose You do complicate things, Jim. Why you count: one, two, three, four – no, I see, you only count the men but that won't stop us telling you what to do, so: one, two, three, four. So: not counting the women, one, two, three –

She comes to James and stops.

Madison We wanted to count all men, Tom, but the Northern states insisted that if the votes of all the men were counted in every state the Southern states would have a vast advantage over the North in the number of its representatives.

Jefferson That would be no bad thing. These Northern States still hanker after a king, I hear they even want a central bank.

Madison Quite, but the South's advantage in numbers comes from its slave population, particularly in Georgia and the Carolinas.

Nelly Rose (*across*) Speaking of numbers, George, you still haven't told us how you make two hundred cherry trees look like four.

Madison (*over to Jefferson*) The Northerners objected, pointing out that since slaves were private property they could count their own horses.

Jefferson Surely no such thing was said by men of reason?

Nelly Rose You can't reason in Philadelphia, it's too hot.

Betty You must have longed for the shade of your trees, Mr Mason.

Madison (*over and fast, to Tom*) If, however, we counted only the free population for the purpose of voting then the South would be vastly outnumbered and have too few representatives in Congress, indeed one-fourth of the country, that's the North, their merchants and their bankers, would govern the other three quarters, the South.

Jefferson The day we are ruled by bankers will be a dark day for America.

Madison Quite. This had to be prevented at all costs. Eventually, after much wrangling and sweaty hours –

Nelly Rose Jim, please don't talk about sweat –

Madison (*over, forceful and fast*) A compromise was reached and it was agreed that every free man would be counted as one person, Indians would be excluded altogether, and, for the purposes of representation and taxation, all the others would be counted as three-fifths.

Christian Three-fifths of what?

Madison (*to Jefferson*) Of a person. The Northern states were so interested in the tax benefits that they overlooked the fact this would give the South a huge advantage in terms of numbers and therefore power. The South will dominate the United States of America, Tom, for as long as we can foresee and we'll maintain the agrarian society in which you believe. I knew that's what you wanted.

Christian Forgive me, Mr Madison, you said all the others. Who are all the others?

Madison The slaves, but the Northerners were squeamish about the wording: they're like the British, they'll accept anything as long as it's not spelled out.

Christian When I walked by those closed windows in Philadelphia, I was confident you were discussing how to enshrine universal freedom.

Madison We had to hammer out a Constitution, not an ode to the dreams of man. Without that compromise we risked slipping back into separate states, separate and weak and at the mercy of the British who can't wait to get back their colonies. They have warships ready now.

Christian Isn't America the inspiration for all those who seek freedom?

Nelly Rose (*to Mason*) George, I can't wait a moment longer to hear how your cherry trees disappear.

Christian (*to all*) Mr Jefferson will never allow –

Madison (*over*) I would not speak for Mr Jefferson, young man.

Mason (*to Nelly Rose*) I planted them in such a way that if you stand at the entrance of the house, all the trees are hidden behind the ones at the front and you see only four trees.

Christian Mr Jefferson, you will never agree to a document that calls a man of colour three-fifths of a human being, it's against the first principles of humanity.

Madison The principles of humanity will not survive without the United States of America, that is a paradox of which Thomas Jefferson is well aware – (*To Jefferson.*) We need your support.

Jefferson is manifestly silent.

Nelly Rose Tom lives on Virginian time, Jim, you'll never rush him into any decision.

Christian And when he does come to a decision, it will be the right one, it will be for the principles we fought for.

Nelly Rose Has your family ever grown cherry trees, Christian?

Mason (*to the men*) I have found that public life is like a wind that erodes the meaning of words. And then a man's principles and even his soul dry out at the roots.

James comes on in a hurry but uneasy.

James Mr Jefferson! Harriet has a fever. Sally has asked if you would come to her.

Nelly Rose James, please don't interrupt my son when he is trying to convince Mr Jefferson to do something he doesn't want to. Where is Sally and who is this Harriet?

Christian I will look at the baby if I may, Mr Jefferson?

He goes with James.

Nelly Rose (*watching them*) What a good-looking young man, even if he does ask too many questions, but a few more years in Virginia and a good wife will cure that.

Madison (*to Jefferson*) We also thought you might like to become Secretary of State.

Jefferson Forgive me, please, for my discourtesy, Nelly Rose, but I'm very worried about this baby.

He leaves. A pause.

Nelly Rose I see. That sort of baby. Betty, you're not hearing any of this.

Betty I know all about all sorts of babies, Nelly Rose.

Madison If this gets into the press, it will ruin Tom's political career. We'll have to keep it quiet.

Mason (*to Madison*) I warn you, Jim: I will not allow you to abridge the freedom of the press any more than I will allow you to infringe the right to bear arms or allow searches without warrants.

Madison You'll get your Bill of Rights, George, but we must all be patient.

Nelly Rose Gentlemen, Virginians are one big family, where's the harm for Tom if he adds to it?

Madison The rest of America isn't Virginia, Mother.

Nelly Rose Isn't it your intention to make it so?

James comes back on, followed by Christian and Betty.

James The *asperges* are ready. Mr Jefferson will join you in the dining room.

Nelly Rose (*to Christian*) How is the baby?

Christian I fear she won't live.

Nelly Rose What a terrible loss.

James (*bursts out*) Why no, Mrs Madison, it's only three-fifths of a loss.

Christian puts an arm on James and steadies him.

NINE

Jefferson's garden. Betty and Christian.

Betty You did all you could, I'm sure.

Christian I wanted to save a life. But medicine is a dialogue with the unknown.

Betty Do you love being a doctor?

Christian I certainly need to be a doctor.

Betty And don't you just love and need Virginia as well? Look at those mountains over there, how blue they look, and these rolling hills, doesn't it make you think we live in Paradise? Doesn't it make you feel full of hope? Even if you are sad about the baby.

Christian I come to this garden and sit alone sometimes and wonder.

Betty It's bad for a man to be alone, that's what Nelly Rose says.

Christian I fought for this land but if you ask men to kill or be killed for an ideal then it must be upheld. Forgive me, Miss Betty, I don't mean to talk to you about such things.

Betty That's all right, I know all about killing: I used to collect snails, line them up and then squash them with my foot. I still feel bad about it.

Christian laughs.

You mustn't laugh at me, I've always wanted to be good and kind.

Christian It's good to laugh. Sometimes when I'm sitting by myself, I feel like crying.

Betty Well then, you must have someone sitting next to you all the time.

Christian I am not sure I would like that.

Betty Wouldn't you? That's not kind.

Christian Unless it was next to a girl as pretty as you, of course.

Betty I don't believe you think I'm pretty.

Christian But I do.

Betty Nelly Rose says gentlemen always want to kiss a pretty girl.

Christian Nelly Rose is very perceptive.

93

Betty Does that mean you want to kiss me?

Christian I suppose it does.

Betty You can kiss me if you want to, Christian.

Christian Betty – I have complications in my life.

Betty Nelly Rose says Virginian gentlemen always have complications in their life and a Southern lady is never bothered about these complications. Would you like to kiss me now?

Christian I believe I would.

They kiss.

Betty How soft the air is. Can you smell the sweet perfume of Mr Jefferson's garden?

Christian I believe it's your own sweetness, Betty.

They kiss again.

Betty Nelly Rose says that when a gentleman kisses a girl a lot it's because he loves her even if he didn't know that beforehand but he discovers it as he kisses her. What have you discovered, Christian?

Christian That I want to kiss you again.

Betty I believe that's the same and I love you too because I want to kiss you again.

Betty Nelly Rose says when a gentleman says he loves a girl and she says she loves him then they ought to be engaged. Do you think we ought to be engaged, Christian?

Christian Betty, when I was in Philadelphia –

Betty Philadelphia is a long way away and we're in Virginia, in Mr Jefferson's garden. Oh, there he is! I think he's seen us. Will you speak to him, Christian? I'll go find Nelly Rose and tell her everything.

She runs out. Jefferson comes and sits next to Christian.

Jefferson Sally seems very weak.

Christian She's in mourning but I don't believe she's in physical danger.

Jefferson Childbirth and the loss of children eventually killed my wife. Sally looked just like her last night.

One of those male moments when men can't quite talk.

Loneliness is a terrible thing, Christian.

Christian doesn't answer.

I wouldn't wish it on any man and certainly not on any Virginian, we're such social animals here. My daughter will soon be married and live away from me. My son died when he was an infant. I think I would have encouraged him to take up medicine. I was never good at the detail of anatomy.

I'm left here on my own with my books but I may even have to sell my library.

Christian Not your wonderful library, Mr Jefferson!

Jefferson I'm in severe debt and Congress wants it. I can build up another one . . . You could help me.

Christian I would be honoured, Mr Jefferson –

Jefferson I'm never happier than in Monticello and I have such dreams here. One of them is to build a university nearby – I've begun to make drawings, I'll show them to you. But there's also my duty to this new country.

Christian We need you to keep the ideals of liberty alive.

Jefferson We fought for the chance to build a new country and change history. I suppose I can't shirk my duty. I so love this garden.

Christian You won't allow that clause to remain.

Jefferson I saw that you were with Betty just now. She would make an excellent wife.

Christian (*after a beat*) I'm not sure I'm free – in my heart, that is.

Jefferson I wouldn't dream of delving into your private life any more than you would delve into mine, but may I speak to you as I would to a son of mine?

Christian Mr Jefferson, you've been more than a father to me.

Jefferson Is the young lady from Philadelphia someone you could bring to tea in this garden?

A silence.

Betty will have the plantation down there. It's small and manageable and you can work as a doctor. And it would give me such pleasure to have you as my neighbour. I understand you're estranged from your family?

Christian They didn't believe in freedom.

Jefferson Betty is a true daughter of the American Revolution.

Christian is silent.

It seemed to me I saw you kissing her.

Christian There's something about your garden. I wasn't myself.

Jefferson Perhaps you were more yourself than you know. We can spend our lives finding out who we are, Christian, but a Virginian marries where he kisses. And you'll do me a great favour.

Christian How so?

Jefferson Nelly Rose will be so delighted she'll keep her overly persistent son from forcing me to act too quickly.

Christian You mean you won't support the Constitution?

Jefferson No man can know what he'll do until he's thought carefully about it.

Christian But you'll protect our liberty?

Jefferson I will protect America and America stands for liberty.

Christian I knew you would. Thank you, Mr Jefferson!

Jefferson It's all settled then. Let me be the first to wish you happiness.

TEN

The Maryland farmhouse. Daniel and Martha. A silent moment, all are still.

Imogen I hear the horses! They're here.

Daniel Let us wait and be quiet. Christian will still remember our ways.

Martha I'm looking forward to a little noise.

Christian and Betty come on. Christian takes in the scene and stands still but Betty rushes to them.

Betty Oh, I'm so happy to meet y'all. Nelly Rose says I'm to tell her all about Maryland although Christian has already told me all about you and that you're not supposed to talk too much and I hope that won't be too difficult for me because you see I was taught to talk all the time because that way there's never any awkward silences but I am just fascinated to learn that silence can be a good thing. And you must be dear Imogen, I've always wanted a sister. My mother died in childbirth but Christian is going to fix all that and nobody's going to die in childbirth any more, isn't that wonderful?

Daniel (*kindly, to Christian*) Christian, we welcome thee back into thy home.

Christian Grandfather!

Martha (*to Betty*) And thou art welcome amongst us, child.

Betty Oh thank you! You're so very kind and I want to tell you all about Virginia.

Daniel (*firm*) It is our custom to sit quietly first and find what is the essence of our hearts.

Betty Oh yes, I'm supposed to sit and say nothing for a long time and then say something very important.

Carl Christian comes on, slowly, with Susannah.

Carl Christian I heard the beloved voice of my prodigal son.

Christian Father!

They embrace. Carl Christian coughs badly.

Father, thou art not well. I can ease your cough.

Carl Christian Susannah has a very good remedy she learned to prepare in Philadelphia.

Christian Susannah, you're here . . .

Susannah Yes, I'm here.

Betty Christian is the best doctor in the world, he's already done so much. He studied with Thomas Jefferson's doctor, he can tell you himself all about it and . . . I know all about plants . . . and things . . .

Daniel We have many things to say to one another but we will not know how to listen if we all speak at once. Christian, thine absence has been a long one.

Christian I knew I had been disowned.

Betty Christian was in the Revolution and there's the plantation to look after and all, and – oh, forgive me, I am not supposed to speak and I just wanted to say that what is in my heart is love and admiration for my husband and how y'all have made him that way, so quiet and serious and I love you all for it.

Imogen (*to Christian*) You have a plantation.

Betty Oh yes, but it's very small and it only needs a few slaves to work it.

Imogen (*to Christian*) You have slaves.

Betty They're mine really and I look after them well: we're all one big family in Virginia. Nelly Rose and I want to invite you all to Virginia but Christian did say you wouldn't understand but I'm sure you will when you see everything.

Susannah This family knows all about Virginia, I've described it to them.

Daniel That is not what kept thee from us, Christian.

Carl Christian It is who kept my son away.

Daniel Christian know that Quakers forgive.

Carl Christian And it is I who need to ask forgiveness.

Christian Father, you don't know what I've done.

Carl Christian I read it on your face

Imogen (*to Christian*) What have you done?

Daniel People speak more easily if one does not ask questions. It is enough to listen.

Carl Christian When a prodigal son returns a father must also return to being a father. I was not a father to you because I did not tell you who I was. Like most Americans. I wanted to bury the past but I know now that if you bury your history its roots only spread underground and sprout again, more virulent than ever.

He coughs, he's weak.

Christian, I inherited a life of ease and cruel privilege, not unlike the one I see you entering now.

Betty No, no, Christian works very hard, we're very simple people in Virginia, Christian even simplified his name because it sounded too aristocratic.

Martha Child, learn to be quiet.

Carl Christian Privilege tends to be invisible to the one who is enjoying it, that's what makes it so pernicious. When I finally saw how worthless my life was, I thought I would give it meaning with that powerful idea: liberty. But with those words that sounded like pure water came instead the flow of blood. As it did with thee, son. I see the ghosts in thine eyes.

Imogen You fought?

Christian doesn't answer.

You promised, you affirmed – you wouldn't take up arms!

Daniel A man cannot make a promise when he has no will of his own.

Carl Christian I knew this, but Christian could not. With us, it was the secret police, we did not consider them human but they were as human as anyone, with bodies they valued, breath – but we only saw the future of mankind not the men in front of us. We killed in the name of freedom. I didn't see the contradiction. I had to flee. I boarded a ship as a shattered soul. I found a family of saints.

Martha Ha! I didn't even want to give you water. It took me years to come to like you because even for us, you were too quiet. There – that was in my heart. It's out now.

Carl Christian And I exchanged myself for someone else. If I had told you all this, you might not have been so susceptible to the ideas that lured you –

Christian I was a hothead, I didn't want to listen.

Carl Christian When you spoke of freedom, I was myself brought back into that fever. It occurred to me that perhaps Daniel was wrong. Liberty, the siren song of liberty, filled my heart again. I tried to quell it – and you.
Is it a hope that will come to us again and again or a curse that pierces us through the generations and leads us to more violence and more shattered souls – like yours now.
What is the acceptable limit to action? I know only one thing for certain, Christian: all privilege is the enemy of freedom. Wouldn't it be better to renounce it now? You would be welcome back into this farm, both of you.

Betty Christian can't stay in Maryland, he's a Virginian and Thomas Jefferson needs him there, he's been like a father to him.

Carl Christian Yes, a young man will find another father if the first one does not catch his heart. Have I lost you? I will lie down now. Come to me later, Christian: mine eyes need to feed upon thy face. No, Susannah, stay.

Carl Christian leaves. There is a silence.

Daniel (*to Christian*) Your father's heart opened to you, now listen to yours.

A silence.

Betty Christian and I met in Mr Jefferson's garden.

Silence.

I can recite all the vegetables and most of the plants there.

Silence.

Nelly Rose says the Virginian landscape is very soothing.

Silence.

Do you have landscape here?

Martha Come, child, let us show you our few vegetables.

Daniel You'll find they grow well in silence.

Betty, Martha and Daniel leave. A silence.

Christian Can you forgive me?

Imogen You left us, you broke all of our lives, you even broke a promise – for freedom.

Christian America is free. You look thin and tired, are you all right?

Imogen You also ignited in me a belief in freedom and it's consumed my life from the inside. Will you come back and be a Quaker again?

Christian I'm married to a Virginian.

Imogen Is marriage about forgetting who you are?

Christian (*to Susannah*) What brought you here, Susannah?

Imogen She found us, she was in a bad way. She thought Virginians were looking for her and she was frightened for her child.

Susannah Portia. Carl Christian is teaching her French.

Imogen I named her. And now you can redeem yourself.

Christian I owe you both that.

Imogen Will you promise? But how will I know you won't break that one too?

Christian I wouldn't forgive myself. Is it about the child?

Imogen When you joined the Revolution, you said it was because the British Parliament wouldn't listen to our petitions. Well, the Quakers have a petition now. And your freedom fighters must listen to our petition. It's addressed to the congressional delegates and one of them is James Madison. The petition reminds them that slavery violates the principles of Mr Jefferson's own declaration.

Christian They know that. It will take time.

Imogen They can stop the slave trade today.

Susannah That's all we asking.

Imogen It's not much.

Christian No . . . it's not much. Did you not want to marry?

Imogen Christian, if you fail to get this petition through, the pain you caused your family will have been for nothing, the years I gave up my own life for your beliefs will have been for nothing. If you fail, even being a Quaker will have been for nothing because it will mean that the only way to freedom is more violence and bloodshed. And if you fail, America will not be the promised beacon of freedom but a cesspool of hypocrisy and destruction. If you fail, Christian, my own ghost will haunt you and your family down the generations. Look at me and tell me you will not fail. I want to die knowing that this dream of freedom we held in our hands has permeated American soil, like water, like water.

Christian You're ill?

Imogen Our mother died young.

Christian Cancer.

Imogen Only Susannah knows.

Christian I thought of you all the time I was away. I imagined your life here . . .

Imogen There was no life. Here is the document.

She leaves.

Susannah It is not easy for Imogen to . . . find peace.

Christian Whose is the child?

Susannah By law, the child of a slave belongs to the mother only. There is no father.

Christian Susannah!

Susannah Betty is young, you'll have many children.

Christian Will you let Portia come to Virginia?

Susannah To be the slave of your children?

Christian I never stopped thinking about you. I wrote, there were no answers. I didn't know where you were. Eventually, I gave up. I still love you. I –

Susannah I'm at peace here. Imogen and I are setting up a Quaker school where Portia will be educated. I've found the best of you in your father and sister. I haven't told them everything.

Christian Will you tell Portia about me?

Susannah I can tell her the story of a young shoemaker who came to Williamsburg fired by the idea of freedom. I'm not sure she'll be interested in the story of a Virginian plantation owner.

Christian I was so alone. Betty has a will of iron under those pretty curls. The Madisons are powerful. I was married before I knew it.

Susannah As long as it made you happy.

Christian It made Mr Jefferson happy.

ELEVEN

Susannah and Christian stay a moment as the Chorus comes on.

Chorus
   Wade in the water . . .

   Thomas Jefferson and Christian in the garden. Thomas Jefferson hands back the document.

Jefferson Nobody wishes for this more than I do, Christian, but we have the wolf by the ears, we cannot hold him nor can we let him go.

Christian You blamed the British Parliament for vetoing any attempt to make the slave trade illegal. There are passionate words against it in your own declaration.

Jefferson As you know, those lines were cut from the final version.

Christian The Quakers are asking Congress for the same thing you asked of the King.

Jefferson The Quakers refused to fight in the Revolution.

Christian They do not believe in violence but they do believe in freedom.

Jefferson Perhaps you can't demand one without the other.

Christian Well, I participated in acts of violence –

Jefferson I am sorry –

Christian – for the sake of freedom, doesn't that give me the right to make demands? I promised my sister I would make sure this petition was presented to Congress with your backing.

Jefferson One should never make promises on behalf of a man you don't know.

Christian I thought I knew you.

Jefferson I don't always know myself.

Christian You laid the foundation of this country with your words. Its cornerstone was liberty.

Jefferson You know that if we try to abolish the slave trade now we'll lose Georgia and the Carolinas, and America will fracture. I have to support the Constitution, the whole Constitution.

Christian You're saying you won't even object to the three-fifths clause?

Jefferson For now.

Christian Once something is in a document people consider sacred it's nearly impossible to get it out.

Jefferson We've shown it's possible to break the shackles imposed by the most powerful army in the world with the cry of freedom. This will never be forgotten, but we can't allow freedom to be an experiment that didn't work. America is under threat, Christian: we must defend it.

Christian If you put America before freedom, what is there to defend!

Nelly Rose, Betty, Madison and Mason come on.

Nelly Rose Are you two discussing gardening? What a beautiful afternoon and we have such exciting news.

Christian (*ignoring all this, to Jefferson*) I fell for the principles of your Declaration, for liberty as an inherent and universal right.

Madison Those aren't the words used in the Declaration, you shouldn't fall for what doesn't exist.

Christian (*over, to Jefferson*) I left my home for you, I betrayed every principle of my family for you. I joined a militia because of you and did what I had sworn I would never do, I killed because of you.

Nelly Rose My dear Christian, we do not speak of such things in a garden.

Christian I lost my community for you but I did it gladly and I waved the banner of freedom which you had embroidered so beautifully with your words and now you tell me you're going to unstitch it all!

Mason I understand your feelings, Christian, I share many of them, but you're not behaving like a gentleman.

Madison You want your children to live in a safe and prosperous country, don't you?

Nelly Rose I'm so glad we're speaking of children, because –

Christian (*to Jefferson*) What can I tell my children about this country when you've betrayed it?

Jefferson I won't accept that. I helped formulate the foundation of a country's freedom, I did not promise to make it work in a day. As a writer I was concerned about first principles and the wording of an ideal. I've been asked to become a statesman. I didn't want this, I only asked to look after my garden. A statesman is not a writer whose words express the glorious possibilities or the hope of humanity. A statesman works with the messy and, yes, the grubbier parts of human beings, their fears and self-interest. A statesman keeps a country bound together and if that means some people have to suffocate, so be it. I have taken on this role for a few years and I will fulfil it.

Madison That's the best news I've heard, Tom, so you're decided –

Jefferson It seems so.

Christian (*to Jefferson*) I loved you more than my own father. You leave me with nothing!

Nelly Rose (*to Christian*) How can you say you have nothing when you have everything? Betty, tell Christian what he has, he seems to have forgotten since he's been with those Quakers who, I must say, for a quiet people, seem to make a lot of noise.

Christian (*to Betty*) We'll go back to Maryland and live with my family. We'll go to Europe.

Betty (*laughing*) I'm not as stupid as you think, Christian. I know about Susannah. I'm not going to Maryland. I'm not going to Europe: I'm a daughter of the Revolution.

Christian I promised my sister I would get this petition through. I can't break that promise!

Jefferson (*gently*) You're not a Quaker shoemaker any more, Christian, you're a Virginian doctor.

Christian I can still make shoes. I can go back.

Nelly Rose There is no way anyone is going anywhere, not with Betty in her condition. They say doctors never notice what's going on in their own family. I had to take Betty to Richmond.

A moment, all realise.

Mason This is wonderful news, I invite you and your new family to Gunston Hall.

Madison I'm feeling envious of you, Christian.

Nelly Rose You always felt envious of Christian, Jim, but we'll find you a wife and she'll make you feel better about yourself.

Mason (*to the silent Christian*) And at Gunston Hall, Betty will at last see my vanishing cherry trees.

Christian Your sleight of hand.

Mason It's called perspective.

Jefferson Your sons will be my first students at the University of Virginia. They'll grow up looking at these hills, at this fertile land. Will you deny Virginia to your children?

Nelly Rose Or Jefferson's garden?

Christian looks around, surrounded and trapped.

TWELVE

Chorus You know the rest: some seventy-five years later the call to freedom drenches these very hills in blood.

— We move on, like water, as, across time and lands, the call to freedom rises.

— I breathe freedom, don't cut off my air: Egypt.

— Horiyah.

— In every street the sound of freedom calls.

— They'll call me freedom – just like a waving flag.

— *eleftheria i thanato*   This really will change

— Too often followed by betrayal.

— Just a broken song of freedom and the closing of a door . . .

— But we keep searching: move underground when we must.

— *eta guertzat*   and for us
  zuzentasuna   justice
  deitua izanen da   will be called
  askatasuna   liberty

— While we glance one last time at the rolling hills of Virginia. It's spring. The shad spawn in the creeks, the land bathes in sparkling green and Christian makes a pair of boots in the oblique light of a warm summer evening.

Christian with a half-drunk bottle of whiskey. James comes on.

James I've come to say goodbye, Doc. Mr Jefferson has freed me. *Je suis un homme libre.*

Christian I heard, James. This calls for a drink.

James Sally is expecting another child.

Christian I had not heard. This calls for another drink.

James Sally made Mr Jefferson promise to free all their children. You'll look after her?

Christian Of course. I don't have many patients these days.

James They don't like you because you look after us.

Christian I can still do that at least. And I can still make a beautiful pair of boots. Who's going to do Mr Jefferson's cooking?

James My brother takes my place. That was Mr Jefferson's condition.

Christian As a free man?

James He takes my place. You told me once about people having to take turns to drink at this river.

Christian I said so many things and I still don't know what freedom is. Maybe my grandfather was right and it's only something you can find in your heart.

James No, Doc, it's out there and I know what it looks like. I'm leaving Virginia.

Christian How can anyone leave Virginia?

James I'm leaving America. I'm going to Europe – Paris first, then down to Spain.

Christian You're free. You're going to Europe. What more can a man want? I wish I could come with you.

James You're free.

Christian No, James, I am not free. *Je ne suis pas un homme libre.* My life was a quest for freedom but I missed it along the way. I took the wrong path, got lost, fell asleep. Like America. Close your eyes for a moment, and the prize Freedom vanishes. But you're free! Let's drink. To your freedom!

James / Christian To freedom!

Christian I think you'll need these boots.

He hands over the beautiful pair of boots as the Chorus takes a bow.